Anyone who has attended Rogers Shooting School or has seen our shirts knows that "Be Fast, Be Accurate, Be the Best" is our motto. These principles can apply to marksmanship but they also extend to other facets of this book.

"Be Fast" in shooting doesn't mean uncontrolled haste. It means efficient, controlled speed. It means not wasting time with nonessential motion. "Fast" eliminates procrastination. It is problem solving without hesitation. These concepts can be used in all facets of life.

"Be Accurate" can mean hitting your target whether you are shooting or performing another task. In business there are many goals which must be met with accuracy. Being accurate can also pertain to truth. My father taught us that "you are only as good as your word." As an FBI agent, my accuracy and truthfulness meant the difference between a criminal being convicted or set free.

"Be the Best" speaks for itself. I was raised with very few luxuries but we were always taught that we were the best. Our father expected us to live up to this standard. It was not grounds for conceit, nor was it an anticipation of perfection. We were expected to always try our hardest and do our best at any task, whether physical or mental. His motto was, "if it is worth doing, it is worth doing right". "The Best" also describes people who are noted for some aspect of their lives. They might be champions, heroes, friends, or everyday people who strive to be the best. Throughout my life I have been affiliated with the shooting industry and shooters. I have met many people who are "The Best". I have mentioned just a few in this book but I am indebted to many.

Be Fast, Be Accurate, Be the Best

by Bill Rogers

ROGERS SHOOTING SCHOOL PUBLICATIONS
3041 Faye Road
Jacksonville, FL 32226
904-642-7810

Be Fast, Be Accurate, Be the Best

by Bill Rogers

ISBN 978-0-578-04794-2

First Printing 2010

Published by Rogers Shooting School Publications
3041 Faye Road
Jacksonville, FL 32226
904-642-7810

Contents

Forward

It has been a long time since I first met Bill, but he has been in the practical shooting game from its inception. I first competed in a US National IPSC championship back in 1981 where he was one of the top shooters. I was a new kid on the block, and doing things differently. Bill saw this not as a challenge to the accepted system, but as evolution. And that is what makes Bill unique. He has always been at the forefront of innovation, a trend he has maintained in many facets of his life. As a shooter, instructor, tinkerer, and inventor, Bill's mind has stayed sharp and focused on solving problems, with an eye for perfection that is difficult to maintain for any length of time. I have seen many people come and go in my life but only a few have left a lasting impression. Bill is one of them.

In the beginning there was the holster, which Bill saw as flawed and began a lifetime journey toward improvement that continues to this day. His contributions to the development and improvement of belt gear for law enforcement, military, and sporting use has had no equal, and most likely never will. Bill was the man who brought me into the Safariland family so many years ago, and his influence has had a strong hand in my shooting success. I think back to the holsters I used before my career with Safariland as the "B.C." era and after as the "Modern Times". When Bill looked at what we needed for the job, he developed new materials and manufacturing processes that were light years ahead of anyone else's thinking. This has allowed for better performance in every measurable category. Speed, security, durability, and safety are all improved because of Bill's work.

Bill didn't stop with holsters, oh no. For those of you who don't know, Bill the innovator, has engineered many of the products and concepts used by every modern pistolero. He runs one of the most "cutting edge" shooting schools in the world, where he pushes the envelope of what can and can't be done. His forward thinking has pushed performance for small arms to the highest levels. In an industry where many instructors get by on theory and ego, Bill has managed to do it the right way. Using observation and analysis, attention to detail, and a logical plan for improvement, Bill gets a student to go further than he thought he could. This is what sets a great instructor apart. I can't think of any shooter who Bill and his concepts would not help.

If this is sounding like I think highly of the guy, it is purely intentional. Few have done as much as Bill has already, and I know his contributions to training and product development for the practical, law enforcement, and military shooter will continue for many years to come.

Listen to the man. He knows what he is talking about.

—Rob Leatham

Rob is inarguably one of the fastest and most winning pistol shooters of all time, winning his 15th consecutive 1911 Single Stack Classic / USPSA Nationals in May, 2009. A few of his major titles include 23-time USPSA National Champion, 7-time NRA Bianchi Cup Champion, 6-time Steel Challenge Champion, 6-time IDPA CDP National Champion, and 5-time IPSC World Champion.

Why Write A Book?

At age 62, I have to ask myself why I would want to write a book now about my career and how I developed a method to effectively teach the skill of shooting. Like most bad decisions, I have a friend to blame. In 2008 a good friend of mine, Chuck Julian, a retired Marine and career shooting instructor, was visiting me at my home. I had known Chuck for 20 years and we had shared teaching concepts and philosophies for all of those years. He urged me, "Write a book if for no other reason than to educate your grand kids." I had toyed with the idea of writing a book before, but it took Chuck's insistence to prod me into the project.

There is an old saying that you are not considered an expert unless you hail from at least 100 miles out of town. Further, you are not truly knowledgeable about a subject unless you have written a book about it. Over the last 30 years I have instructed, demonstrated, and lectured at my shooting school as well as all over the United States and selected places in Europe. I occasionally hear my concepts verbalized by others and sometimes even see those concepts written in books and gun magazines. Much of it is accurate but in many cases, just like the party game where you tell someone a story and it is passed around, the critical elements are left out or altered. I think the opportunity to put my knowledge about shooting in a written format so that shooters and shooting instructors can refer to these fundamentals, is the main motivating factor for me to write this book.

An advantage of waiting this long to write a book is that my ideas have been tested over and over. Every concept and theory that I put in this book has been tempered by years of observation and experience. The methods and philosophy that I write about in this book have been tested and perfected by me and my instructors for over 30 years. These techniques are not understood by the mainstream firearms academia. My techniques and teaching philosophies are considered unorthodox by most and objectionable by many. However, I have taught thousands of average people shooting skills that the mainstream firearms instructors consider impossible. My students continually outperform their peers in simulated and real life scenarios.

From the late 1970s to the early 1990s I competed in shooting handgun and three gun matches sponsored by USPSA- IPSC, the Bianchi Company, *Soldier of Fortune* magazine, and the NRA. I earned numerous state and national titles and was ranked in the top 10 shooters in the world. I was the first person to "clean" the Bianchi mover in competition and the first person to complete a 3 second run on the Bianchi Plate event. There are a lot of gifted competitive shooters around that have equal or better shooting skills than I. What makes me qualified to write a book about shooting instructions is that I am not only a skilled shooter, but for over 30 years I have instructed thousands and thousands of people from all walks of life; men and women of all races and all different skill levels. I have taught at my school and other police academies. I have taught many young people as young as 12 years-old and shooters on the north side of 50. Because my school is solely owned by me, I can change the entire format tomorrow if I wish, just to see if it will make a difference. In the past I have done just that, changed what I was teaching almost overnight when I was convinced there was a better method.

I'm writing this book in hopes that those who are interested in advancing the life-saving shooting skills of our police officers and our military forces may "see the light" and update the archaic and obsolete ways that they administer firearms training. There is no other option, except more mediocrity and irrelevant training.

At the Rogers Shooting School, we have always used a series of tests that the students must undergo to graduate. Most other private shooting schools use subjective criteria to award levels of skill to their graduating students. Our students actually must perform and meet a standard. We use nine individual tests in the handgun program.

There are a total of 125 possible points. Each student takes all nine tests each day of a five-day program. A student that achieves 70 points passes the program. A score of 90 to 109 points guarantees the student an "Intermediate" rating and 110 or over is required for an "Advanced" rating.

Most students who are highly rated by other shooting programs, especially local and federal law enforcement academies, have difficulty passing our basic program. Much of the reason is because what they have learned at other shooting institutions is counterproductive to our training and most real-life gun battles. Most of their prior experience has been precision or point shooting. Their subconscious minds are not prepared to deal with small, partial targets that are moving and exposed for only the briefest of moments.

It takes much more training to recondition a shooter's subconscious mind before he can begin to learn reactive skills. This is why I believe that it is imperative that the present day shooting academies change the way they teach a new shooter. Some instructors believe that they can "scale" the drills in order to teach their students how to speed up their shooting. They start off with the target exposure set at a certain speed and then after many repetitions they speed the program up, thinking that this is the way to teach their students. This method counters everything that is known about reactive training. It is also a serious waste of resources. If you start out with a goal to teach someone to hit a head sized target at 30 feet in a half second, you should not begin by giving them 1.5 seconds to accomplish that goal. Reactive skills are learned by the subconscious mind through repetition. With the target exposure set at 1.5 or even 1 second, the student's subconscious is trained to rely on that time to accomplish the drill. When the target exposure is decreased we must reprogram the subconscious mind to deal with the shorter time. It usually takes at least three times more repetitions to retrain the mind than it would to train the subconscious at the correct speed to begin with. Instructors that teach skeet, trap, or sporting clays do not start out by slowing the speed of the targets. Someone trying to learn how to hit a fast ball at 85 miles an hour does not start out with slow pitch soft ball. Unfortunately, most of the administrators who control the law enforcement and military firearms training programs are blissfully unaware of what they don't know. My hopes are that this book will challenge these administrators to question their present teaching policies.

For over 30 years, I have offered to show any agency how to change their shooting program to better prepare their students for real-life combat with firearms. Unfortunately, most see my program as "extremely advanced" and insist that basic firearms training must be taught beginning with slow-fire. The real truth is that my program is not "advanced" for students who have been taught correctly from the beginning. It is, however, very advanced for someone who has been incorrectly trained from the beginning.

Personal Background

I was born just after the Second World War. My family consisted of my mother, father, and two older brothers. We grew up out in the country near a little town of Lockhart, Florida. We lived on a clean, clear, spring-fed lake that was connected to two other lakes that covered several square miles. There was 60 acres of orange grove next door to our house and a small pond that was part of the grove. Four huge avocado trees grew in a central portion of the orange grove.

My father was medically retired from the Air Force as a full colonel with a 100 percent physical disability. He had been a pilot and the commanding officer of the highly successful and decorated 90th Bombardment Group. The "Jolly Rogers," as the unit was named, fought the Japanese with B-24 Liberators from a base in New Guinea. Earlier in my father's youth he had been an avid bird hunter and a competitive skeet shooter. He had been a member of the U.S. Army Air Corps Skeet Team. At the start of the war, he was instrumental in the development of shotgun shooting from gun turrets mounted on Jeeps. He believed that this was a great teaching aid to help the aircraft gunners learn the fundamentals of shooting at rapidly moving targets. His group had the highest ratio of downed enemy fighters to loss of bombers in the Pacific Theater.

While living in the jungle of New Guinea, he contracted a disease that had no cure or effective treatment at the time. At the end of the war he was basically sent home to die. However, he proved the doctors wrong and continued to fight the battle against the disease. I recall him spending several weeks a month convalescing on the couch in our living room. My father rarely left our home. He was there when I got up in the morning and was there when I went to bed. Because of his health, he supervised our tasks rather than doing much of the labor himself. Due to his military career he ran everything much like the Army. He was a harsh disciplinarian. He demanded honesty, integrity, loyalty, and hard work. My brothers and I believe that he stayed awake at night planning every project for the next day so that we would not be able to finish until sundown. In the late 1950s one of the modern miracle drugs gave him some periods of relief from his illness. He succumbed to his several afflictions is 1984.

Because of my father's modest income, we grew up living by our wits. We had a fairly complete machine shop and our father taught us most of the basic skills of machining and welding of metal. We did odd jobs, light machine work, and bought everything used and rebuilt it. By any standard of the time we would have been considered poor, but we did not know that at the time. We grew fruit, vegetables, flowers, and plants for resale. We had access to all the oranges and avocados we could eat. We fished in our lakes, shot dove in the grove near the pond, hunted quail with our dogs, and lived with freedom that unfortunately our children and grandchildren will never experience. Just the thought of an 8-year-old boy out at night alone, with a handgun hunting varmints, in this day and age would cause hysteria among our liberal society.

We lived in an era long forgotten. We went to the county fair and spent our hard-earned money at the "shooting gallery." We paid 25 cents and the attendant handed us a loaded Winchester Model 1890 .22 pump rifle. The sweet smell of expended powder and the sheer simple joy of knocking over moving, miniature, steel animals will never be experienced by my grand kids. During that era, as kids, we carried pocket knives to school, walked or rode our bikes several miles from home alone, and weren't afraid to talk to strangers. Our doors did not have locks and we left the keys in the ignition of our cars. We played dodge-ball at school and actually kept score at all the games we played. We learned at a very early age that sometimes you won but many times you lost. We learned how to deal with a defeat without whining or crying. Loosing simply offered us a challenge. We further learned that if you really worked hard and practiced a lot at a skill, your chances at winning improved. We understood that no one was entitled to a house, a car, food, clothing, a job, or health care. You had to earn everything through hard work and responsible decisions. People who were successful were admired. We aspired to be successful. Our present "entitlement" society is taught to revile successful people and businesses, and to believe they should be punished by taking a greater share of their wealth for society's good. "People" not profit is the new world slogan. "Hope" and "change" is the new philosophy which has replaced "determination" and "perseverance" of my era.

Some families we knew growing up played horseshoes or croquet after church on Sunday. We shot guns. My father's flight surgeon during the war retired from the Air Force and opened a medical practice in nearby Winter Park, Florida. He visited our home almost every Sunday when I was growing up. He was our family doctor as well as a good friend. "Uncle Larry," as he was fondly known to my brothers and me, was a true "gun nut." He loved firearms and collected them for most of his adult life. He would regularly bring over a new pistol or rifle on Sunday and after we competed by busting old potatoes, tin cans or clay targets, we each would take turns firing a few rounds from a beautiful, brand-new firearm that we perceived as a piece of art work.

My duties, which I cherished, were to field strip the weapon and clean it to its original pristine condition after we finished shooting. I would spend an hour or more alone, meticulously cleaning and reassembling the coveted firearm. Learning about and understanding the workings of the intricate mechanisms of firearms at an early age gave me the background that has helped to guide me through my career in the firearms industry.

Living where we did, very isolated in the country, we were plagued by vermin and critters. At certain times during the year, the citrus grove would become infested with rats, raccoons, and opossums. We had four acres of manicured lawn that the armadillos would ravage. We had a dense population of gar fish in the lakes that preyed on the minnows of our favorite game fish, the large mouth bass. The simple solution to these problems was through the skilled use of a firearm. In most cases, a trusted .22 Long Rifle pistol was the desired choice. My two favorites were a Colt Woodsman and an S&W K-22 "Combat Masterpiece". Both were wonderful guns.

Although we had rifles, most of our varmint hunting was done with handguns. Most of our shooting was done at night with the use of flashlights and sometimes dogs. Shoulder weapons were too cumbersome. Because the support hand was being used to control the dog or the flashlight or both, only one-handed shooting techniques were employed. Almost 20 years went by before I learned two handed handgun techniques. At night, gar fish would swim very near the surface feeding on minnows. My middle brother would drive our boat and I, with a flashlight in one hand and a pistol in the other, would shoot and kill gar by hitting them in or near the head. I killed many a gar with that trusted old Colt Woodsman. We would bury the gar in my mom's rose garden for fertilizer. Of course we would use shotguns when bird hunting, but that was about the only time we used shoulder weapons.

Armadillo Hunting

In remembering my childhood and the use of a rifle, I have to tell the story of the Jungle Carbine and the armadillo. I turned 9 years old in March of 1956. When I did, it became my responsibility to deal with the armadillo problem. We had four acres of grass that had at one time been an area to cultivate flowers, vegetables, and other plants for resale. My father had directed us to maintain this area now as a manicured lawn. One side of the lawn bordered a neighbor's property and had been unattended for many years. It was primarily rough brush and briars. The armadillos lived there and at night they came onto our property and ravaged the lawn, eating earthworms and grubs. Several nights a week I would advance to the area near the rough brush with a Rayovac 6 volt spot light in one hand and a trusty Colt Woodsman in the other. I would move at a stealthy pace with the light off until I could hear their movement. I would move as close to the sound as I could before turning on the light and engaging the enemy. In a short period of time, the armadillos recognized that the light was followed quickly by gunfire as I ran after them. Many people believe that these critters have tiny brains and are really very dumb. I have a great deal of respect for their survival instincts. I came to believe that they had developed an intelligence network of informants that allowed them advance warning of my attacks. On many occasions I would slip through the darkness and discover that they were nowhere to be seen. The following morning I would find further destruction of the yard that was my responsibility to repair. I began altering the times that I would search for my prey. If I woke up in the middle of the night to go to the bathroom, I would take the opportunity to search the yard. I could get by with firing my .22 at night during the winter months because the windows were closed, but during the summer I was not allowed to wake the family. Over several months I had no success in a confirmed kill of an armadillo, probably due to my inability to successfully hit one. However, on more than one occasion I was sure that I had hit one with at least one shot due to their erratic movement after my shot. However, somehow they were always able to run to the brush area and crash their way into obscurity. I was convinced that the standard velocity .22 Long Rifle cartridge was just not capable of penetrating the beast's armor and causing a fatal wound.

I rationalized that they were probably running off in the brush and dying later but somehow their population continued to grow.

In June I convinced my dad that I should be able to buy a rifle with my own savings. I ordered a British Enfield .303 Jungle Carbine from the NRA. I can't recall the price but it was exorbitant at the time. I probably paid less than $30.00 for it. It came in the regular mail in a wooden box and included two boxes of ammunition. The rifle was covered with a form of grease. I cleaned and polished the metal and refinished the wooden stock. I coveted that rifle. I would ask my dad each week if I could shoot the carbine during our regular Sunday matches but he would put me off by saying that the carbine would be too loud and would disturb the neighbors. He also said that it would be necessary to build a deeper back stop because of the power of the cartridge. He told me that in October when we went bird hunting we would take it with us and we could shoot it then. The cardboard ammo boxes had a label that referred to the bullets as AP rounds. I asked my father what this meant and he told me that is stood for armor piercing.

Then there came that fateful Sunday morning. I woke early just at first light. There was a dense fog over the yard that was just beginning to lift. I looked out through our porch window and saw a large armadillo still digging away at a site. I could make a shot from the doorway with a rifle without ever going into the yard and alerting the enemy. It was almost day break so surely I would get a pass for waking up the family, especially if I bagged an armadillo. To insure my success, I now owned a rifle and armor piercing bullets. I was convinced that this was the ingredient that I had lacked in my missions up to now. I figured I would have some answering to do if I fired a shot from inside the doorway before anyone else was awake. Since I was going to be in trouble anyway, I might as well use the Jungle Carbine to insure my success of killing the armadillo. A dead armadillo would go a long way in mitigating any punishment. If I missed the shot or if the armadillo ran away wounded I would be in a world of hurt. I had never shot any rifle cartridge except a .22 Long Rifle. I had shot a 20 gauge shotgun during bird season and I knew that it had quite a kick and made a lot of noise. I compared the British .303 cartridge to the cartridges that I was familiar with. It was a lot bigger than .22 Long Rifle, but it was also a lot smaller than a 20 gauge shotgun shell. I surmised that it must be louder than the .22 but have a softer kick than the 20 gauge. I carefully bolted closed the carbine and opened the porch door. I took a deep breath, sighted through the peep sight at the armadillo, and began to press the trigger. I was correct on the first assumption. It was louder than a .22 Long Rifle. We did not know about ear protection in those days and if you are familiar with the concussion associated with high powered rifles, you can imagine my surprise. That surprise was only surpassed by the kick that was associated with the blast. The Jungle Carbine had a very hard rubber butt plate that might as well have been made of solid wood for the amount it cushioned the recoil. I was wearing nothing but jockey shorts. There was nothing between me and that hard rubber butt plate. My dad immediately came running from his bedroom armed with a .45 pistol and shouting obscenities. The rest of the family had begun to barricade themselves. Apparently World War III had begun without warning. When the smoke and fog had cleared and the inquisition began, I had three things going for me. One, there was a dead armadillo in the yard; obvious proof that although the critter may be resistant to .22 Long Rifle bullets, it's armor was certainly no match for a British .303 AP bullet. I certainly had a heightened respect for the cartridge. Secondly, my father was so relieved that he was not actually engaged in a gun battle on an early Sunday morning that he might not beat me too much. Thirdly, and probably the main reason for leniency in my case, was because I had a black and blue shoulder that corresponded with a black and blue cheek. My dad, when he finally passed judgment, was so angry that he could hardly speak. He told me to go bury the armadillo, and then to repair the five foot long trench in the yard that the .303 had created after passing through the varmint. He then told me never to shoot my rifle near our home again. I followed all orders as prescribed and counted my blessings. For many years though I was convinced that a .303 British Enfield AP round was necessary for dispatching an armadillo. As I think back to this real story what is amazing to me now are the freedoms that we once had. Imagine a 9 year old buying a military rifle with ammo through an ad in a magazine and receiving it in the mail. That all changed when Lee Harvey Oswald used a similar purchase to assassinate President Kennedy. And as is always the case with restrictive gun laws invoked by the government, they are only obeyed by the innocent law abiding citizens. Those laws did not prevent the shooting of President Reagan many years later.

Developing Reactive Shooting Skills

My brothers and I realized that in order to improve our skills, we needed to practice at shooting targets that represented our real challenges. All the varmints that we encountered around our homestead, without exception, would be moving when we turned on the flashlight or at least when we began to shoot at them. Raccoons and armadillos would many times take a hit from a .22 and continue to fight or escape. Follow-up hits on an erratically moving animal were often necessary. For this reason, we concluded that shooting at a stationary target was simply a waste of time and ammo. We intuitively recognized that we became more skilled when we were able to instantly recognize a hit on the target.

When we hit a varmint, the effect was instantly recognized. Paper targets, thin aluminum cans and plastic bottles would not give us the instant feedback we desired. Chipped and discarded milk bottles would have been our favorite choice, but the cleanup of the broken glass made them prohibitive. Discarded potatoes, charcoal briquettes and balloons were tried, but we finally settled on targets that we made from broken clay birds recovered from the local skeet and trap club.

We built molds in our machine shop that worked like a waffle press. We used an old, converted linotype furnace and filled it with broken targets that the local trap club was happy to have us pick up. We would open the valve and the melted substance would flow into one of our molds. It would quickly harden and we could remove the target, cool the mold in water, and start the process over in a few seconds.

We could attach these targets to fishing line and swing them from a frame, or we could launch them from a gravity runner. The runner was just a pulley connected to a wire cable suspended from two telephone poles. From the pulley we could extend a line with a clothes pin attached. We attached one of our clay targets to the clothes pin and positioned the target at the high end of the telephone pole. We secured it with another clothes pin connected to a line that one of us was holding. When the shooter was ready, a yank on the securing line would start the mover.

We were not allowed to engage it until it was half way through its run downhill and still accelerating. When the shooter did things correctly, the target would explode in bits of black particles. The pure glee and exhilaration realized when we turned one of the targets to black dust is still a fond memory of my childhood.

We eventually built a trap that threw targets similar to a conventional trap thrower, but we shot those targets with shotguns. In time we got into reloading shotgun shells and we began to shoot clay targets that we had made. In the 1960s, Remington came out with the "Power Piston" shotgun wad. We learned that we could pick these up at the local gun club when we were picking up the broken targets. We ran them through a laundry washer and dryer. We reloaded the shotgun shells with the used wads.

Later we bought a small portable gold mining pump and sluice in order to recover lead shot. The trap club was closed to shooting on Wednesday when we would pick up broken targets and wadding. The trap range looked out over a small lake. We used a small inflatable boat, bought from surplus, which we rowed out about 30 feet into the lake and started the Briggs engine on the gold mining pump. In minutes we had filled the inflatable to its maximum capacity with lead shot. We cleaned the lead shot, dried it, and recycled it with the used wadding. The first 100 straight trap targets that I broke at 16 yards was with this recycled shot and wads, and a JC Higgins 12 gauge shotgun. At 14, I was the Junior State Trap Champion of Florida. A few years later I helped finance my way through college, shooting the Calcutta Handicap events during the Winter Chain Shoot that took place in Florida. The Calcutta was a big-stakes gambling affair and I made money by betting on myself.

The FBI

I married my wife Christie, who remains my wife to this day, as a senior in college. In 1969 I graduated from the University of South Florida with a degree in geology. I applied for a position as a Special Agent in the FBI, a goal I had worked toward since high school. At the age of 22, I was one of the youngest men to be selected for training at the FBI Academy in Quantico, Virginia. I was intrigued about the possibility of becoming a Special Agent like the one portrayed on TV by Effrem Zimbalist Jr., but the main reason I was lured toward the Bureau was because of their firearms training program.

At that time, the "Practical Pistol Course" , "Hogan's Alley", man-on-man dueling, and the "moving man" course were considered state-of-the-art firearms training for the FBI and select elite law enforcement officers from around the world. I arrived at the FBI Academy in July, 1969. Thinking about it now, I was just a kid. I had only been out of the state of Florida for two short trips and had never seen snow.

The Bureau, as we learned to refer to our employer, the FBI, was under the direct leadership of J. Edgar Hoover. The Bureau fell under the "command" of the Justice Department, but there was no question for whom we worked. There was some controversy then— and a lot more after his death— about how Hoover ran the Bureau. No question, Hoover was dictatorial. He was a harsh disciplinarian. He required a strong work ethic. He demanded you be squared away with short hair and conservative dress and that you embody the tenets of honesty, integrity, and loyalty. Hoover did not believe in giving anyone a second chance for disobeying orders. You would not embarrass him or the Bureau. I loved it. I was right back at home.

The 16-week training period at the Academy was a blur. I enjoyed practically every aspect of the training and my time at the FBI Academy. If it were not for the fact that I missed my wife and new-born daughter, it would have been one of the best times of my life. I was, however, disappointed with the firearms program. Much of it was slow-fire on stationary cardboard and paper targets. We shot only once on the Moving Man Range and that was with rifles. We shot once through Hogan's Alley, and the last day of firearms training we shot a single elimination, man-on-man dueling exercise. With the exception of skeet, everything else was static paper.

The S&W Model 10, 4-inch barreled revolver was our issue weapon. We were issued a "Hank Sloan" leather holster made by Bucheimer-Clark. We shot one-handed and were taught to shoot from either side of a barricade with either hand. The shooting was easy, but the things that were new to me were working from a holster and "hip" and "point-shoulder" shooting. I knew very little about these skills. My brothers and I had tried to emulate Marshal Dillon of "Gun Smoke" by trying to hip-shoot some targets, but we found the technique did not work well when a wounded raccoon came screaming down a tree to tear up our favorite dog.

Back at the academy, I quickly learned the skills of drawing and point-shooting at close-up targets, but the remaining instruction was not a real challenge. To teach shotgun manipulation, a conventional skeet range was used. The first day our class attended the skeet range instruction, one of the instructors demonstrated each position before the class would follow him through that position. He was having difficulty hitting the targets and after the third station of observing me shoot, he asked me to do the demos for the class.

We had one instructor, Al Booth from Plant City, Florida, who was an exceptional shooter. He was the epitome of what I expected a firearms instructor to be. That is not to suggest that the other instructors weren't qualified, but Al was just outstanding. He believed in being able to demonstrate the skill he was trying to teach. He taught me a lesson that I use to this day— you must be able to successfully demonstrate a difficult skill in order to motivate your student to learn that skill. He had grown up around firearms, much like me. We bonded immediately and we remain friends to this day.

Just after the second week of our 16 week course, we were introduced to the Practical Pistol Course. It was a timed course, shot on a stationary, man-sized cardboard target. The target was engaged from 7, 25, 50 and 60 yard distances. Hip shooting was required at the 7 yard line and the shooter was allowed 25 seconds to draw, fire five rounds at the target, reload and fire an additional five rounds at the same target.

Upon completing the hip shooting phase, the shooter moved to the 60 yard line. At the 60 yard line, with the weapon loaded and holstered, a timed event began that concluded after 5 minutes and 35 seconds. The shooter was required to shoot five rounds from prone at the 60 yard line and then move to the 50 yard line. At the 50 yard line, the shooter fired five rounds each from sitting, prone, standing behind a barricade right handed and then left handed.

The shooter then advanced to the 25 yard line where the target was engaged with five shots with the shooter kneeling and then standing behind a barricade, right-handed and then left-handed with five rounds each. The target had a five point area named K-5, which represented the area of the head, heart, lungs and upper stomach. The remaining area of the torso was worth four points per hit just outside of the K-5 zone. A peripheral shoulder hit was worth three, and the lower arm earned you two points. Below the waist tallied three points and peripheral hits on the body were given one point.

The course was shot with 50 rounds of ammunition loaded from your pocket and 250 points was the maximum possible score. You were given 10 attempts during the 16 week course and you had to shoot two scores over 65 percent in order to qualify and become a Special Agent. On July 28, two weeks after starting the academy, I shot for my first time the famed FBI Practical Pistol Course. I only shot two shots slightly out of the K-5 area, into the K-4 zone, for two points off a "possible." My score of 248 was better than each of our five instructor's score with the exception of Al Booth, who shot a "possible" or 250 out of 250.

Our instructors had years of shooting experience. They were selected as the best of the best. They were astounded at my score. They asked me how I had learned how to shoot that well at my young age. I told them that I grew up shooting gar from a moving boat and raccoons and rats out of avocado and orange trees. To me, shooting at a big paper target that did not move was not all that hard. That was probably not the politically correct response, but it was the truth.

Shooting a great score early in my stint at the Academy opened another door that ultimately paved the road to my success as a holster inventor. The chief armorer at the Academy was a true Virginia gentleman by the name of Lester Limerick. Each afternoon after shooting, we would clean our revolvers and turn them back into the armory. When the half-door was open to receive the guns, I would look past the clerk signing in the guns and feast my eyes on the milling machines and gunsmiths working. The man that ran that shop was my "Wizard of Oz." I asked several times if I could just enter and look around for a brief time, but I was told that there was no admittance for the likes of me.

That all changed when I shot 248 points. Lester heard about my score and he also learned about my interest in his shop. One afternoon he invited me to have a look around. Lester was responsible for purchasing practically everything that dealt with firearms for the Bureau. He was also responsible for the reliability and accuracy of all the Bureau weapons.

Our issue revolvers employed fixed sights. If they did not shoot "point-of-aim/ point-of-impact," they had to be corrected by gently bending the barrel in the frame. The actions sometimes had to be tuned, or timed, so that the cylinder would carry up to the bolt stop position before the hammer would fall. If the hammer fell before the bolt stop position was reached, the result was lead spitting out the gap between the cylinder and the forcing cone and an inaccurate shot. At the same time if the hand was forcing the cylinder past the bolt stop position when the hammer fell, the same negative event was the result. Lester took the time to explain these gunsmithing skills to me. We became friends and I was in his debt at the time, but later in my life he increased the balance owed by 10 fold.

To shoot a "possible" during your career as an FBI Agent was a coveted achievement. Normally, you only had one chance a year to shoot a formal PPC match toward winning the "possible" award. The event had to be witnessed by a supervisor to count. If you were ever successful, you received a cash award, a letter from the Director, a medal, and your name was engraved on the granite wall outside of the gun vault at the Academy. No one could recall a student shooting a "possible" during training school.

That became my goal. However, that goal evaded me. I became ill with the flu and then pneumonia during the last several weeks of the Academy. In fact, I even missed the class photo. I shot several very high scores but because of my illness, I did not shoot the last four of my 10 qualifying PPC matches. I passed all my written tests and qualified with all of the shoulder weapons and was shipped out to Oklahoma as a "first office agent."

I arrived in Oklahoma City as a first office agent and I was assigned to a squad supervised by an old curmudgeon, a crusty, old-school, former Marine, cigar-smoking, ass-chewing, disciplinarian. His name was Travis Muirhead. For the slightest lack of good judgment, he would shove all the files off his desk, verbally cuss you out for half an hour, and threaten to fire you on the spot. I loved him. Agent Murhead knew what was right was right and what was wrong was wrong, which was exactly how my father had raised me.

The Agent-In-Charge of the firearms program was named John Harrison. John was also old and crotchety and not well liked by many of his peers. He believed that the Agents in his office should qualify at the range with the weapons they actually carried on duty. Agents could carry a personal firearm if it was first inspected and approved by Lester back at Quantico, but it was necessary to have approval also at the local office. Many liked to carry the five-shot S&W Chief's Special snub nose. Many did so without qualifying with that handgun, which put them at odds with John.

During my first week in the office, John called me in for a conference. He noted that he had reviewed my file and had seen that I was a gifted trap and skeet shooter. He wanted to know if I would travel with him on the weekends and shoot the major trap events in Oklahoma. He pointed out that Oklahoma was the only FBI office that had number 7½ shot 12 gauge shotgun shells in its inventory for training (this load is used primarily for trap shooting). I had died and gone to heaven. That year I became the State Champion of Oklahoma and John was runner-up.

It is ironic how select events and certain people shape your life. I had no desire or intention to ever teach shooting skills when I entered the FBI and yet the random chance that sent me to Oklahoma helped to alter my life. Two shooting legends of the time lived in Oklahoma. One was D.A. "Jelly" Bryce. He was a famous and retired FBI agent who had killed a number of villains in his line of duty as an Oklahoma City police officer and later as a FBI agent. He was also an exhibition shooter, performing all sorts of shooting feats. Unfortunately for me, he had all but given up shooting before an audience by the time I arrived in Oklahoma. However, many of the old-timers in the office and in the police department had witnessed his exhibition shooting feats. I would listen to anyone who would talk to me about Jelly Bryce.

Another famed exhibition shooter was Captain Dan Combs of the Oklahoma Highway Patrol. Fortunately, I was able to witness a shooting exhibition by Captain Combs and talk with him briefly about his techniques. Both Bryce and Combs were very gifted and all-around accomplished shooters. They could perform quick-draw. They were capable of point shooting, hip shooting, and hitting hand-thrown aerial targets with handguns and rifles using solid bullets. Dan referred to his techniques as "spot-shooting" and many of his concepts are intermingled in my own techniques which I will explain in later chapters.

In the Oklahoma office, we shot a lot during our firearms training sessions. We shot the .45 ACP Thompson submachine guns, shotguns, and our service weapons at every session. I believe that because of Bryce, Combs, Harrison and the pervasive firearms culture of the Oklahoma office, we shot more and took firearms training more seriously than we ever did later in my career.

Around October 1971, I was transferred to the Chicago office of the FBI. First office agents were only allowed to stay a couple of years at their first assignment. I really liked Oklahoma and the people I worked with. The selection process of the FBI insured that the people you worked with were exceptional. I think if I had been allowed to stay in the Oklahoma division, I would have retired there. However, I believe one's destiny in life is directed by a higher authority. I moved my wife and child to Chicago. Chicago was a big office with hundreds of agents.

The criminal squads were much more specialized than what we had in Oklahoma. There was so much crime that the U.S. Attorney's office only concentrated on the major cases. For this reason the quality and complexity of the cases were different than Oklahoma. We did not work stolen cars and many of the other cases with which the Bureau had joint jurisdiction with other agencies.

With almost 100 banks in the downtown area, we had several bank robberies every Friday night. Since bank robberies were still a major crime that the FBI investigated, the robberies provided a major case load for the Chicago office. We had seven criminal squads in the office so we rotated squads each week to work the robberies that occurred every Friday night. Every seventh week, you could count on working several bank robberies on a Friday night and sleeping over at your desk before catching a train home some time on Saturday.

The work was exciting and the people I worked with were great, but the commuting and harsh winters were difficult. As far as firearms training was concerned, Chicago was very different than Oklahoma. We had access to an indoor range where we shot during the winter months and we had a couple of sessions a year outside at a Navy range facility north of the city on Lake Michigan. Most of the agents looked at firearms training as a necessary evil. At every session on Lake Michigan, ammunition was left over because most of the agents shot just the minimum requirement. I would build simple target systems that offered some fun and challenge to the shooting program, and a few friends and I would shoot until the extra ammo was all gone.

On September 22, 1972, I shot a "possible" during a regularly scheduled qualification shoot. The rules were that you had to have a supervisor witness the entire event and sign off on your target. I approached the Agent running the training program and asked if I could have a re-shoot with a witness. He agreed to witness the course of fire, in case I could shoot another "possible." I shot a back-to-back "possible" and received the coveted award. My name was carved on the granite wall at the Academy.

Around the time that I shot the "possible," I began working on two projects during my off-hours. The first was a target system to learn Dan Combs' techniques of "spot-shooting." In my basement I mounted a 50 inch tall roll of brown craft paper on an axle standing up vertically. Eight feet away I had built a similar axel with just the cardboard core. This "take up" core was driven by an old rotisserie motor. The same motor could be quickly inverted and connected to the main roll to rewind the paper.

I built a backdrop behind the area made of a half-inch thick piece of dense felt. The paper was pulled from the main roll and wound onto the take-up spool. Once I started the motor, I used a marker to draw about two-inch diameter circles at different intervals and different heights. After six spots I would leave an open space to provide a time interval to reload. I would create about four episodes before I would change the motor and rewind the paper.

After rewinding, I would again change the motor and ready the target system. I used Speer plastic cases and bullets, a reloadable casing fired by only a primer which fired a lightweight plastic bullet. The bullets were accurate to about 50 feet. After I loaded my revolver with the Speer cartridges, I would holster my revolver and start the motor. The speed was such that I had just enough time to draw and engage each spot before it disappeared. Thus I began my journey to discover how to "hip shoot" a small moving target.

The First Kydex Holster

My second project was to develop a better holster. Both a partner and I, during two different arrest situations, had experienced a loss of our revolvers from our holsters. Both times the weapons were retrieved with no further harm, but the failures started me on a quest to build a more secure holster. At the same time, my "spot shooting" basement experiment directed my interest to design not only a more secure holster but also one that would aid in hip shooting techniques.

Berns-Martin had developed a leather holster that used a wire form that held the revolver in a clam shell style covering. The draw was accomplished by working the wrist and rocking the revolver through the front of the holster. The natural position after the draw was a hip shooting position. I decided that I would improve on the Berns-Martin design.

An office rule in the Bureau was that if you had your jacket off in the office, your revolver needed to be secured in your desk. Most of us felt awkward walking around with an empty holster so we would normally take the holster and weapon off and stow them in our desks. To put the holster and revolver back on required undoing our belt, positioning the holster, securing the belt, and tucking in our shirts. This re-dressing while female clerks and stenographers were present was also a bit awkward.

I decided to design a front-break holster that could be clipped on or off the belt without first undoing the belt. I was not experienced with

First plastic formed holster that I actually wore for almost a year as an agent. It was not made of Kydex but of General Electric Noryl. Circa 1972

leather or spring wire. As a youngster I had worked with fiberglass and polyester resins. The first holster I built was made of fiberglass. It worked about two weeks before it cracked. Fiberglass was not an optimal material for a number of reasons, but I was intrigued about how thin, lightweight, and strong a holster could be made using a plastic material.

I began to research and try different thermoplastic sheet materials. My first success was a material made by the General Electric Company called Noryl. It formed at relatively high temperatures but it was strong and resilient. I made my first real carry holster from this material and carried my service revolver in it for almost a year. The Noryl was folded around the revolver and part of the spine of the holster continued up and curved behind the trigger guard. The revolver was securely clamped in the formed sheet material and the revolver could not be drawn up and out like a conventional holster. It had to be rocked forward and driven out through the front opening. I named the design a "front break" holster. My wife, Christie, convinced me that I should apply for a patent on the design, which I did. The first all-plastic holster, patent # 3,902,639, was filed by me on November 21, 1972. The holster had a formed "back piece" that slipped inside the trousers and it had a metal tab affixed to the back side of the holster that locked under the bottom edge of a dress belt. Because it looked a bit like a ping pong paddle, it quickly became known as a "paddle holster."

I continued to research plastic materials until I came across a brand-new plastic extruded sheet material manufactured by the Rohm & Haas Company. It was called Kydex and it was a wonderful material. It was a PVC-Acrylic alloy. It formed at lower temperatures than the Noryl and it was less likely to break at re-curve areas of the holster that had to continue to flex. These were the areas associated with the paddle and the trigger guard lock. After working with Kydex for a short period of time, I settled on its use exclusively.

During a weekend, if I did not have too many other chores, I could build two or three holsters which I sold to members of my squad and others in the Chicago FBI office. By the first of January 1973, I had a fair number of orders for my lightweight, front break, paddle holster. To help sell the holster, I would invite Agent friends over to our house. Once in the basement, I would load up with the Speer plastic bullets and turn on my reel-to-reel target system. As the spots would come passing by, I would quick-draw from my holster and hip shoot a hole through the paper. I was never in the league of Jelly Bryce or Dan Combs, but I was impressive and I could sell holsters.

In February 1973, I was called back to the FBI Academy for "In-Service Training." It was a normal course to return to Quantico where the in-service Agent would meet with Bureau administrators to discuss future career alternatives in the FBI. I looked forward to this opportunity because my goal had now changed. I wanted to come back to Quantico and change the Firearms Training Program to a more realistic, dynamic model. I wanted multiple moving targets. I wanted targets that would appear from cover and disappear quickly. I envisioned targets that would react to being hit and targets that the students would be required to continue to engage and hit until the target finally succumbed. I wanted humanoid targets that represented only a small visible portion instead of a large frontal depiction of a facing man.

These were not totally original ideas. These were the ideas and concepts of Combs and Bryce and even went back to Col. Rex Applegate of the OSS during World War II, but they were the epitome of the real-world experiences I had gained throughout my life. With the exception of Jelly Bryce and a few other famous Agents, the FBI had not fared well in shoot outs with criminals. I believed I could make a difference and I believed my ticket to this new job was my shooting ability and my new holster invention. Surely the administration back at Quantico could see the merit to these ideas and would want such a person to implement them.

The Rogers Holster Company

Upon arriving at Quantico, I called on my old friend, the Bureau armorer, Lester Limerick. I told him of my plans and goals and showed him one of my new holsters. He was impressed with the design, but he cautioned me about bringing up such radical ideas about changing the entire firearms program. After all, this was a huge government bureaucracy steeped in tradition and not likely to change due to the efforts of a 26-year-old Second Office Agent. Lester was a wise man. My meeting with the administrative supervisors did not go well. I was basically told to go back to Chicago and mind my own business.

I was demoralized and very unhappy. I dragged myself back to Chicago and the winter seemed worse than ever. Several months went by and I got a call from Lester. He said that he really liked my holster that I had left with him. He had been unable to convince the firearms staff to make my holster an issued piece of equipment, but he had the authority to issue the holster to National Academy students. The NA, or National Academy, was a program that chose selected police officers from around the country and around the world to attend a 16 week training program much like the program for FBI agents.

Lester said he had an open purchase order for 400 holsters and that I needed to find a company that could fill the order and soon. He told me that it would be a conflict of interest to buy the holsters directly from me. Besides, I could only produce about three holsters a weekend. I made up samples and sent them out to all of the holster companies I could find. I included a letter that explained the purchase order. I wish now that I had kept the replies. They would have been priceless pieces of history. The polite ones said things like they were not skilled in working with plastic and did not believe that it was a medium that would ever be acceptable in the holster industry, especially for law enforcement.

I was in trouble. I called Lester with the bad news. He suggested that I request a leave of absence from the Bureau and start a holster company. If things did not work out, I could go back to work as an agent. I was not yet 27-years-old. I had two small children and a stay-at-home wife. I still had payments on a Opel Kadett car and very little savings.

Nonetheless, Lester's suggestion sounded like a great idea to me. In retrospect, the idea was ludicrous. Now I understand why my wife Christie cried a lot at night. I wrote my letter requesting a leave of absence from the FBI to pursue a project that would benefit the Bureau. While waiting weeks for a reply, I received another call from Lester. The holster I had left him had worn off some of the bluing on a test revolver. I would have to line the holsters with suede leather.

A number of adhesives would work with gluing suede to plastic or other leather, but with my process the plastic patterns had to be heated to 350 degrees Fahrenheit before they could be formed. None of the conventional adhesives could stand the heat. It was almost impossible to glue in a lining after the holster was formed. I was in trouble again. As I was pondering what seemed an insolvable problem, I recalled a

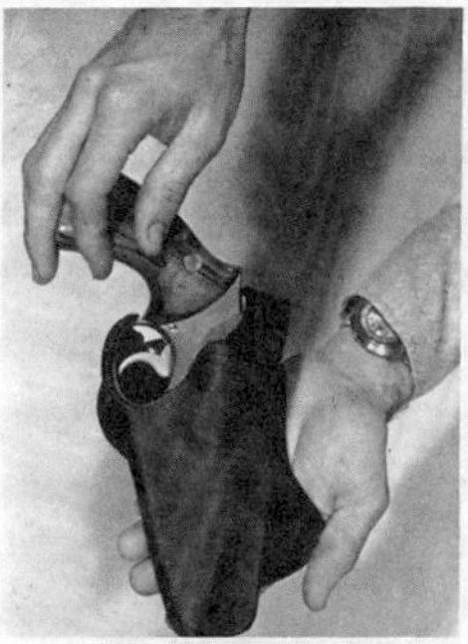
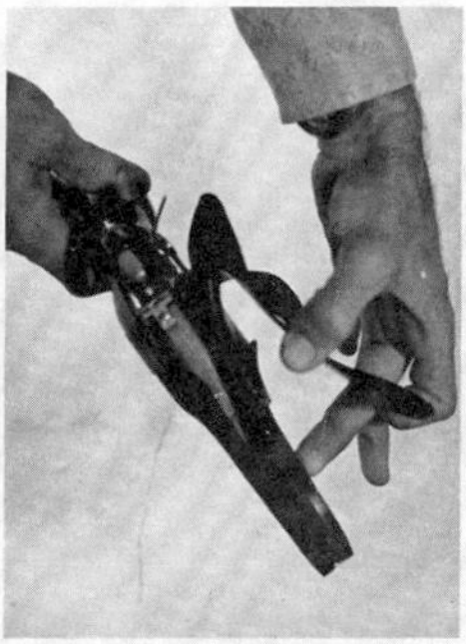
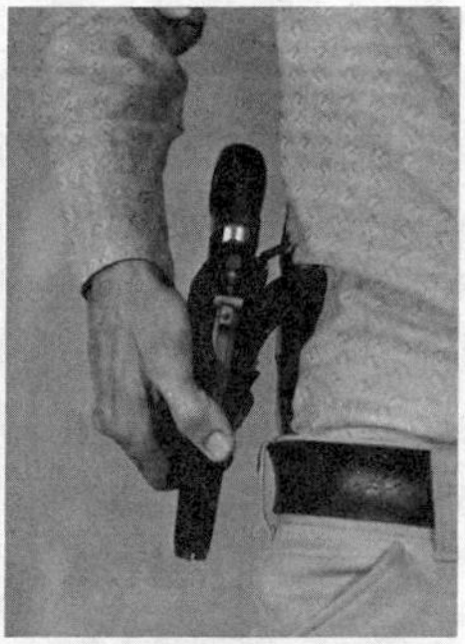

To put the holster on; the intended wearer should place the contoured back flap inside the waist band of his trousers and, while flexing the holster shell outward from his body, push the holster down until the one way lock on the back of the holster shell has gone below the belt.

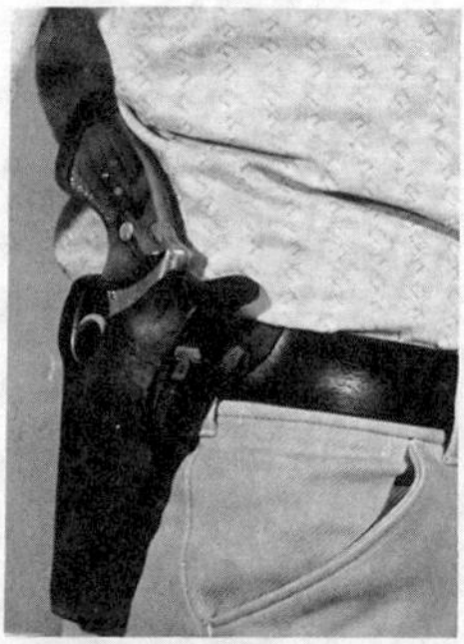
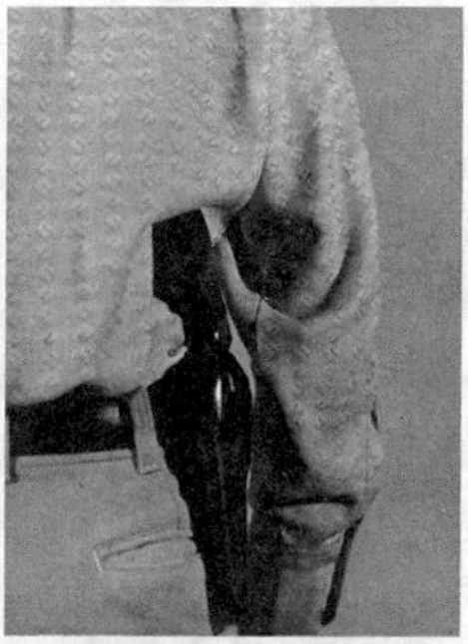

* *The tough, synthetic material used permits a design that holds the pistol close into the body, leaving a profile that approaches the concealment qualities of an "inside the belt" holster.*

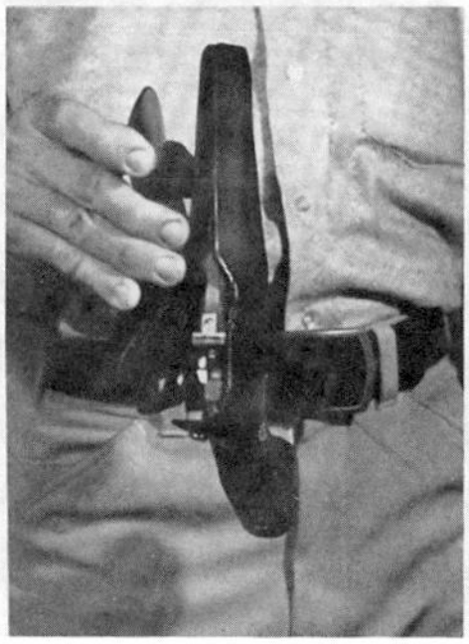
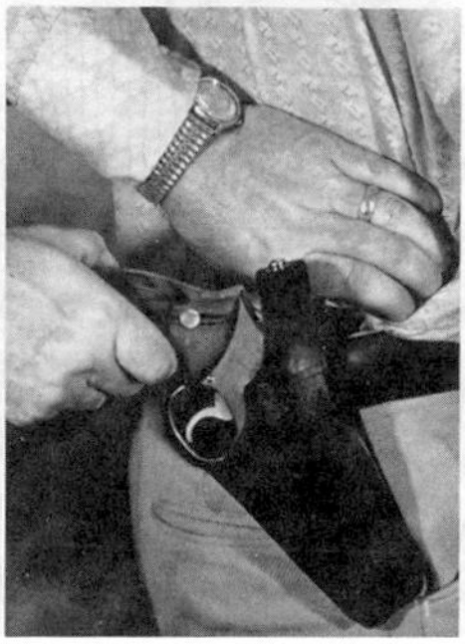

* *This holster uses a unique design feature that prevents the pistol from being dislodged from the holster while running or tumbling. To draw the pistol, a force must be applied to overcome the built in tension and holding design. A thumb snap, single movement, release is used in some models to prevent even this action, thus making the pistol impossible to remove unless intended by the wearer. In either model – with or without the snap – a pistol cannot be drawn up out of the holster from behind.*

First production, Kydex paddle holster sold to FBI – 1973.

case that had caused me to investigate a truck tire remanufacturing company. Because of my fascination with anything mechanical, during the investigation I had became fascinated with the process of "vulcanizing" the caps on old tires. The process used a Nitrile rubber solution in Methyl Ethyl Ketone. The solution was applied to both cap and tire core and allowed to dry.

The Nitrile rubber would attack and bond itself to both surfaces. Once dry, the two parts could be pressed together without sticking. However, when you brought the temperature up to 300 degrees and added some pressure, the two parts became one. I refined the process and made it work for laminating leather to the inside and outside of the plastic core holsters. I was back in business. The process became known as "thermoplastic and leather laminate" or simply "thermolaminate," and it led to another patent.

I received my authorization to leave the Bureau for a maximum of three years with the agreement that I would pay for my move back to Chicago if I left the area in the meantime. I would miss the great people I worked with and the prestige that went with the job, but I now had a personal mission to accomplish. I sold my house, loaded up the kids and Christie in the Opel Kadett, and moved back to Florida.

A college friend of mine had an injection molding and plastic fabricating business in Jacksonville. He and his father invited me to start up the holster business in a small section of their building. With the equity I had from the sale of my home in Illinois, I bought a small three bedroom house. I rented it out for a little more than the monthly mortgage. I moved my family into a two bedroom apartment. I bought a Honda 350cc motorcycle so my wife could use the Opel. I formed the Rogers Holster Company and hired a single employee, a lady named Teri James.

In six weeks, I built forming presses, convection ovens, and other custom tools necessary needed to build the holsters. Teri and I made the 400 holsters for Lester. I made sure each holster had a readable logo including my address. We were paid promptly and I had a little working capital, but things were really slow. My buddy was in the process of buying his father's business. He offered me a partnership. I recognized a lifeline being thrown to me and accepted. I was now the Rogers Holster Company, a division of Alpha Plastics.

And then it happened. I began getting requests for my holsters from all over the world. The NA graduates from the FBI Academy

First Rogers's duty holster with leather laminated to the outside, circa 1975.

were impressed with the holster Lester issued to them. I received purchase orders from the Thailand National Police, Scotland Yard, NIS, OSI, CIA, and the RCMP. Orders were coming in from everywhere. I could hardly tool up fast enough. My part of the business grew and I was able to buy the holster company division clear from Alpha Plastics. It was now the Rogers Holster Company and I owed much of my new found success to Lester.

By now I was up to about seven employees and was making the payroll each week, but that was about all. The Bureau job back in Chicago was looking better and better. I realized that I only had one product, a concealable paddle holster for revolvers only. This was not much of a product line to launch a lifelong career.

I quickly designed a uniform duty holster which was just a beefed-up version of my paddle holster with a fixed back piece to accept a Sam Browne duty belt. I began traveling around, calling on police departments, and trying to sell my new-fangled plastic duty holster. I was not well received. This was 1974 and the uniform police agencies were steeped with traditions of leather and Bill Jordan style Border Patrol holsters with conventional straight-up draws and forefinger release snaps. My holsters were black plastic with a "hair cell" finish. We may find it amusing today as the same material is now commonly used, but in the 1970s my holsters were derisively dismissed as "Mattel holsters."

I had to do something and do it quickly. I remembered my sales pitch in my basement in Chicago and I decided that what I needed was some "sizzle" in my sales program. I made up several small, round, steel plates that had a foot on them. I threw a take-down saw horse in the back of a pickup truck and I headed south to call on police departments. I would introduce myself to the sheriff or police chief of a department. I would tell them that I needed to show them a new holster, but that it was important that I do it in a live-fire exercise at their range.

I think they were more curious in what I had up my sleeve than they were interested in buying a new holster, but most of them took me up on the offer. I insisted on having their head firearms trainer present during the event. Usually by the time I had set up my saw horse and positioned my steel plates, I had several interested witnesses, including the chief and head instructor. I would hand out stop watches and ask the volunteers to start the watches when the chief said "Fire." I explained that upon the command, I would draw a revolver from my holster and hip-shoot down three steel targets. The watch operators were instructed to stop the watches when the last plate fell.

The distance I used was between 7 and 10 yards. My times in those days were under 2.5 seconds for the drill. I normally had to do the drill over several times before I got the volunteers to operate the stop watches instead of just staring in awe. Believe me, I was no Dan Combs, Bill Jordon, or Jelly Bryce, but I looked pretty good. Once I got the time established, I would then turn to the head instructor and ask him to do the same drill. He would invariably make some excuse, but in almost every instance the sheriff or chief would insist that he participate. Most departments of that era had no mandatory time for drawing and hitting a target. Many still do not have such a requirement. As you would predict, the instructor would struggle with his draw, somehow fumble his gun out of an old-style leather holster and usually empty his revolver before knocking over any of the metal targets. At that point I would step up and talk about how my holster gave me the unfair advantage over the instructor's obsolete, piece of junk holster. It was an argument that the chief and instructor were willing to listen to. Surely this brash young holster maker could not be a better shooter than a seasoned firearms instructor! The technique worked for a while until a chief in south Florida called me one day and said his department had bought my holsters and his officers still shot like crap.

The Boss Holster

My holster designs evolved in a short time and I realized that a true "security" holster was something that was sorely needed. Studies had shown that almost 20 percent of the police officers killed in the line of duty during the '60s and '70s were killed with their own handguns. This was 1975 and all police handguns were revolvers.

I developed a simple test that could be used by any department to determine if a holster was a Security Level 1, 2, or 3.

The test was to mount a chosen holster on a volunteer's gun belt. We then locked up the appropriately double-checked unloaded handgun in the holster. A second individual had five seconds that he could use both hands to grip the handle of the handgun or the holster and pull violently in any direction without the wearer resisting. The attacker in the test was instructed not to intentionally release any securing device that the officer would use to release the weapon. The force was directed at the holster body or the gun itself. After five seconds of violently yanking, jerking, tugging and twisting the weapon and holster, the attacker would stop and the wearer of the holster was instructed to accomplish a draw in under two seconds.

If the handgun remained in the holster and the holster remained on the officer and if the officer could draw in two seconds after the attack ceased, then the holster was subjected to a final test. The holster was unsnapped and the wearer rocked back on the ground as in a reverse summersault. If the handgun remained in the holster after this final test, it was rated as a "Level 1" security holster. No one else in the industry had proposed any type of security test. This test was my own idea and I simply used common sense and experience to establish the parameters of the test. I was aware that there was no governing agency that would adopt such a test nor was it likely that any of the other holster companies would recognize my test standards. I developed the test for only one reason. That was to determine what duty holsters on the market were able to pass the test.

I began testing all of the available duty holsters that were on the market and found that none of them, including my own holsters, would pass the first portion of the test. Most of the handguns literally popped out of the test holsters with the first yank. Other holsters simply tore off the belt, leaving the wearer totally unarmed. The "Safety Speed" holster, which was a hinged clam shell design, seen on the popular TV series, CHiPs, would usually contain the weapon but if you twisted the revolver in the holster, it would jam the holster so that we had to use a hack saw on the metal latch to recover the revolver.

I went to work to build a lightweight holster that would pass my Level 1 test. During this era, the Uniform Crime Report had statistics of how many officers were killed with their own handguns, but there was no information of how the officers lost their weapons. Most of us in the holster industry incorrectly assumed that the officers were losing their handguns from rearward attacks that were difficult to defend. I, like John Bianchi and a few other designers, concentrated on developing holsters that offered more protection from rearward attacks.

I took my original "front break" design and beefed it up considerably. I developed an injection molded "spine" that captured the rear curvature of the trigger guard and connected to the muzzle of the holstered revolver. That molded piece was riveted into a thermo-formed molded clam shell container that fit the contours of the revolver. This formed shell used the "Thermo-laminate" technology that I had developed and patented.

The thermo-forming, or injection molding of plastic holsters, is common today, but in the early '70s, wet-formed leather with spring

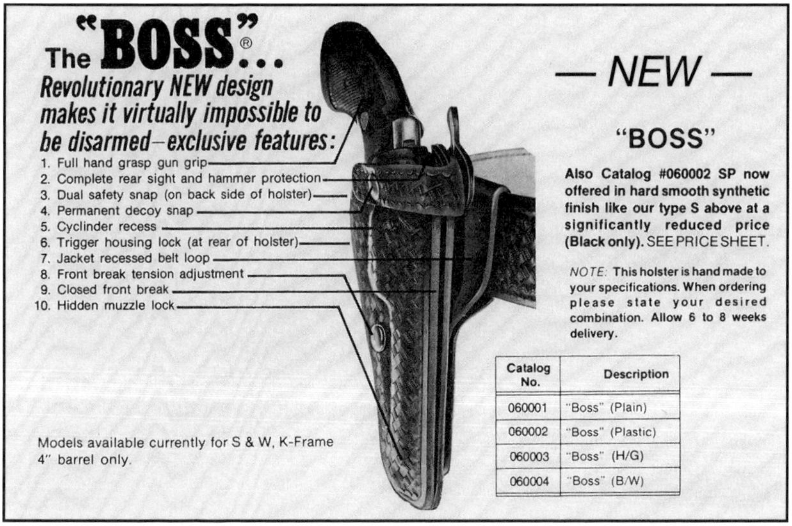

Boss holster - 1977

wire forms or stamped metal parts was the state of the art. To keep my designs from being derided as "Mattel," I used my patented process to laminate leather suede on the inside and finished leather on the outside. Most customers did not even know that the core of the holster body was plastic.

Unlike the competition's leather holsters that used spring wire or stamped metal inserts, my holsters would not change shape or stretch when they got repeatedly wet. After several months of trial and error and hundreds of "violent assault" gun-take-away tests, I finally developed a holster that would pass my Level 1 test. Because of the very strong injection molded spine, the revolver could not be drawn from the rear by an attacking adversary. It could not be drawn out the front as long as the clam shell was locked closed by a retaining strap. The mechanism that released the strap had two modes. The normal mode was a thumb tab that, when operated, lifted the strap snap off of a stud to release the strap. The second, more secure mode allowed the operator to deactivate the thumb tab by snapping the strap under the tab. The operator had to release the strap by thumbing a much smaller tab at the end of the strap.

The holster was light years ahead of the industry. I named it the

"Boss" and it became famous. It not only passed all of the requirements of the Level 1 test but also it would still lock the revolver up from a reward pull, even if the securing strap was released. I considered this a requirement of a Level 2 holster and thus I established the requirements for a Level 1 and a Level 2 holster. If a holster could pass a Level 1 test and still have a degree of security with the primary securing device released, then it was a Level 2. I now had the only holster in the industry that would pass a Level 1 and also a Level 2 test.

I called the "Boss" a "security" holster to differentiate it from regular "duty" or "uniform" holsters. I should have applied for copyright protection for the term as it has become synonymous with most of my holsters. My rating system and testing protocol was published by the Rogers Holster Company and distributed to every department considering new holster purchases. When I was invited to show my holster before a purchasing committee, I insisted on having all of the competitors' representatives present when I did my demonstration. I would buy all of the competitors' holsters in advance and test them. I knew their weakness before the day of the demonstration.

At the demonstration I would ask each representative to put on their respective belt gear and to secure an unloaded revolver in their holsters. If a representative refused, I would simply ask an attending officer to wear the representative's holster. I would line up all the reps with their holsters on and would perform my Level 1 test, being careful that I did not ever apply any force to anything but the grip of the revolver.

Most of my competitors' holsters failed the first pull and none of them lasted close to the five second mark. When I had finished destroying all of the other holsters, I would calmly invite each of the offended salesmen to conduct the same five second test on the holster I was wearing. By this time in the demonstration, there was a lot of pent up anger among the reps. I would return home that night with bruises, strained back and leg muscles, but in over 40 demonstrations, I never lost a revolver during a Level 1 test.

At industry shows, I would do the same demonstrations and invite anyone in the crowd to come forward and test my holster. I also would perform my famous "water test." I had a 2.5 gallon aquarium filled with warm water on a stage. I would place a competitor's leather holster in at the same time I would place my holster in beside it. At the end of my take-away demo, I would take the two holsters from the aquarium and mount them up on belts. My holster would work flawlessly. Within a few draws, the all-leather holster would be stretched so far out of shape that you could usually pull the revolver from the holster while it was still strapped up.

I was not a well liked man among my holster designing peers. The "Boss" holster was truly a superior design, but my company was very small. I did not sell through the standard distributor organizations. I did not have sales reps and I was my only salesman. Also then, just like today, much of the sales of a product to a government agency were based on political or personal connections and not the virtues of the product.

I was just making payroll and my take home pay would barely buy my family groceries. I had started a bullet and ammunition business as well as a steel target and shooting school business that were helping to pay the bills. By May, 1976 my business was still struggling and I was considering "pulling the plug" and trying to get my old job back with the FBI when I received an invitation to show the "Boss" in Canada. Again, the old adage of a person not being an expert unless he is from out of town, proved to be true. I was well received in Canada and so was my holster. The only problem was that the agencies in Canada were instructed to buy certain products that were made in Canada.

I worked out a deal with a Canadian company that would assemble the "Boss" in Canada. My company would make all the parts and ship them to Canada, where they were assembled, tested and delivered. In the end I won a contract to supply the "Boss" holster to all the law enforcement branches of Canada. The "Boss" was the issue-holster for almost every unit until the semi-auto pistol became prevalent. From that point on I never looked back.

I have told people for years that I never really left the FBI. I just took a leave of absence and never returned. The sale of the "Boss" to Canada and the success of my shooting school during the first few years of business gave me the necessary capital to expand and to spend more time researching new problems and developing new solutions.

The SSIII Holster

In early 1983, I became interested in learning more about how officers lost holstered weapons during a fight. I asked for help in my quest from friends in the FBI and others from several of the state investigative agencies. I requested all the information available about any incident in which an officer lost his weapon during a fight. In many incidents, the officer survived the attack or was not shot after the assailant gained control of the weapon. In those cases, I received permission to interview the officer to learn more about how the loss occurred.

What I found was that in an overwhelming number of incidents, the attack and resulting loss of the sidearm was initiated from the front or side of the officer— not from the rear. There are several reasons for this. Primarily, most officers rarely allow a subject to get behind them and intuitively turn into an act of aggression. Within six months I had investigated two take-away incidents from officers wearing a "Boss" holster. In both cases the officers had released the securing strap before the assault. Both assaults came from the front and because that was the direction the holster was designed to release the revolver from, it was easy for the assailant to grab the gun out of the holster.

I was disheartened. The "Boss" was a good holster, but I had designed it to be secure from the wrong direction. I immediately set off to design a holster that offered protection from the front instead of from the rear.

I also had studied numerous cases where the securing strap was released by the officer prior to the attack or by the assailant during the attack. My desire was to design a holster that would have two securing straps, a primary and a secondary. I wanted the primary strap to be obvious and require a deliberate action by the officer. I wanted the secondary securing strap to be concealed and to be intuitively released when the officer acquired a shooting grip on the handgun. The result was the most popular security holster— if not the most popular duty holster— ever made.

The design used my Thermo-laminate and thermo-forming patents to make a semi-clam shell that opened from the rear. The holster was formed in such a way that it locked up on the top cylinder ledge of a revolver or the ejection port ledge of a semi-auto pistol. It had two securing straps. The primary strap came over the top of the handgun and was released by a conventional thumb tab. A second strap was attached so that it went around the body of the holster and secured with a snap behind the holster between the holster body and the belt attachment piece. There was a small tab that was released by the operator's middle finger while forming a shooting grip on the handgun.

I found that the holster would pass a Level 1 test starting with both straps secured. It could pass another Level 1 test with the primary strap released and with both straps released, it still offered a great deal of security during an assault from the front or the side of the officer. I now had established the definition for a Level 3 holster. I named the holster the "SSIII," short for Security System Three.

For the first couple of years it was a hard sell. It was considered too difficult to draw from and was labeled a "widow maker" by those agencies that were still using the open-top, single-strap Border Patrol style of holster that would not even pass a simple Level 1 test. The normal reaction was summed up by a sheriff in a small county of Georgia. He drawled, "That's a pretty neat holster, son, but I don't have nobody smart enough in my department to learn how to draw from it."

My competitors openly mocked the design and there was numerous articles written about how dangerous the holster was because of its complexity. I had invented the most advanced security retention holster ever made and most observers thought I would never sell it, especially to law enforcement agencies. Many acknowledged its advantages, but thought the design was too complicated and required too much training. Now I had a holster that required not one, but two straps to be released and then the handgun still had to be manipulated in a special manner in order to draw the handgun out.

My competitors were dancing in the street. I showed the holster for almost a year without having my first sale. Finally, I went back to my old trick. By this time, with the help of my brother, I had developed the first range timer. It was called the "ERT" for Electronic Range Timer. You could easily dial-in a set time in tenth of a second intervals and it had a random start button. I would invite the chief or sheriff and his range instructors to their range. I would set up two saw horses with one 8 inch diameter steel head plate on each one. I would go through a complete demonstration of my SSIII and I would then invite anyone to do a take-away test.

After that I would then challenge any instructor or other officer

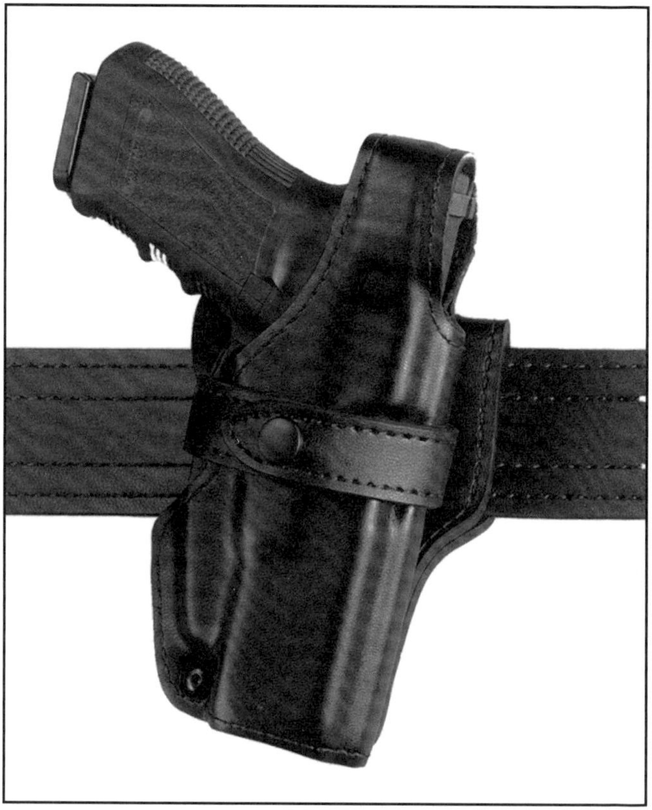

SSIII – Patent issued September 22, 1987.

there to a holster duel with me wearing an SSIII that had just gone through several security tests and them wearing whatever holster was issued by their department. During my demonstration I had done everything very deliberately and had not performed any quick draws at all. It was not difficult to get a challenge from the range instructor staff. They were sure it would be an easy victory in their favor.

I would have someone start the contest with a random start signal from my ERT. The contest was to see who could draw and knock over their steel head target first. The distance was about 20 feet from the targets. In over 40 such duels, I never lost a contest. Word quickly got around to the point that no one would challenge me for fear of looking stupid.

But this level of confidence in my product was what caused the departments to begin to consider the SSIII. In much of the same way that Richard Davis of the Second Chance company sold vests by shooting himself while wearing one, I began to sell some holsters to departments that were progressive in their training and concerned about officer safety in a struggle.

My first big sale was to the Orlando (Florida) Police Department. This was especially rewarding because I had grown up in a little town near Orlando and had graduated from high school there. I had outdueled the department's firearms instructor, Frank Repass, and he was determined to learn how to use the holster as well as I could. The end result was that he trained his officers how to draw and shoot better from the SSIII than they could from what they were presently using.

Orlando proved to be a big success story and within a year several large agencies in the country were training with the SSIII. It followed the "Boss" holster in Canada and became the issue-holster in that country. The model SSIII (and later the same model designated as the model 070 by Safariland) has been in constant manufacture for almost 30 years and has proved to be, so far, the most successful safety holster ever built.

At one time, before Safariland bought my company, I had a file with over thirty letters from officers who believed the SSIII holster had saved their lives. I suspect that the more recent SLS and ALS holsters that have been designed since 2000 by my company and manufactured by Safariland will eventually overtake the SSIII, but it was the SSIII that set the standard for all other safety holsters.

The Rogers Shooting School

In 1976 I had worked out a lease with a local FOP shooting range and began to do some contract handgun training primarily for police officers. The instruction was based around the use of my duty holster designs and concealed holster equipment. The instruction was all one handed and all the close shooting (under 10 yards) was done hip shooting. I did offer some classes to the civilian population but the instruction was more tactics than actually teaching them how to hit a target.

In 1977 a firearms journalist and well-known shooter by the name of Ken Hackathorn called me and asked me to use my design talents to make a top-draw holster for the 1911 .45 ACP pistol. I told him that I had just designed a "front break" design for the 1911. He said that the kind of shooting he was involved with did not favor hip shooting or a front-break style of holster. He told me of a combat style of a sport shooting that had originated in California by the Southwest Combat Pistol League. He said that in May of 1976 a loosely-knit body of shooters who participated in this new bred of "combat shooting" had met in Columbia, Missouri and had formed an organization. It was called the International Practical Shooting Confederation, abbreviated as IPSC and pronounced "Ip-sick."

Ken told me about the favored style of using two hands and bringing the weapon to eye level. He described a push–pull method called the Weaver stance. A combat style of pistol shooting that did not favor hip shooting? I was more than curious. I offered to pay his air fare to Jacksonville to show me this new type of shooting. He arrived and we went straight to the range. He had a simple cardboard target with scoring zones. He said that each drill was scored by taking total points shot on the target divided by the time to shoot the drill. After this final math calculation was done, the person with the lowest factor won the match. The scoring system was known as "Comstock scoring" after Walt Comstock, a member of the Southwest Combat Pistol League.

By combining the points on the target with the time it took to shoot, the Comstock method was a blend of speed and accuracy. It made sense. Ken started with a single target about 7 yards away. On my command, he drew a custom built 1911 .45 and shot two shots in the center of the body of the target. He brought the pistol to eye level and used two hands, but his left elbow was bent (a shooting style which had become known as the Weaver technique.) I used a stopwatch to time the event. He did it several times and I noted the scores and times with pencil and paper.

I now did the same drill while he timed me. I was hip shooting one-handed using an S&W Model 19 from my front-break holster. To his surprise, my times and hits were very close to his. To my surprise, my hip shooting was no faster than his two-hand-held pistol brought up to eye level. He proceeded to add another target and our results were very competitive. Then he made his point.

He placed a target around 7 yards and another to the side about 10 yards away. On the 10 yard target, he placed a white "no shoot" target in front so that only the head of the shoot target was visible. His time between targets did not vary. I could hip shoot the first target, but I could not transition to the "hostage" target without bringing the revolver to a point-shoulder position and index on the front sight. The difference in time was staggering.

I didn't have to shoot another drill. Ken was right. Within a month I had bought a Colt 1911 .45 and had mastered the Weaver technique. I began to travel and shoot in matches around the country. In my second match, I went to Berryville, Arkansas and shot a match put on by a young gunsmith named Bill Wilson. I didn't win the match, but I placed very close to the top. I was shooting a stock Colt 1911 with small thumb safety, short trigger and dinky, stock sights. The prize I won was a custom combat conversion supplied by a local hotshot, the gunsmith, Bill Wilson.

I left my stock gun with Bill. We became good friends and I have shot his custom guns for over 30 years. We became partners in developing and selling gun parts. He and I became vise presidents of the newly formed United States Practical Shooting Association. We served together for many years as Area Directors on the USPSA Board of Directors.

The enlightening demonstration by Ken Hackathorn, followed by my involvement with USPSA-IPSC motivated me to produce an entire product line around the sport of IPSC. I produced a line of speed holsters, belts, and magazine cases. My first IPSC holster was the "Combat Competition" model followed by the "Edge". In a short time the Rogers Holster Company dominated the shooting sports that required holsters for pistols. In 1981 the Rogers Holster Company produced three models of IPSC holsters, Hackathorn, Wilson, and Plaxco. These were holster designs that each of those three shooters preferred and they became the most popular holsters of the IPSC sport during that era. They were built using the formed Thermo-laminate Kydex-core process with a fine grade of leather on the outside and soft suede leather on the inside. The first 100 of each model were numbered and signed by hand. A few years later I introduced the famous 007 holster which because a Safariland product. I established a shooting team made up of myself, my wife Christie, Tom Campbell, Bill Wilson, and Mike Plaxco. Later, as my company transitioned from Rogers to Safariland, top shooters like Rob Leatham, Jerry Barnhart, and others were added. To this day the Safariland Company has followed my lead and continued to sponsor a shooting team competing in most of the handgun sports. Safariland has continued to offer a line IPSC holsters from the 007 to the present 013.

My involvement in competition shooting rekindled my desire to teach shooting. I had instructed my wife, starting with someone who had not grown up shooting and she had quickly become a national as well as an international pistol and revolver champion. I now believed I had a mission in life to quickly and efficiently teach others how to shoot using the new methods I had learned. My goal became to teach police officers and military personnel these new shooting techniques. I believed I had discovered the best way to convey these principles and techniques.

I had figured out that there was an element common in my own experiences and what I had learned about Dan Combs, Ed McGivern, Ad Topperwine, Herb Parsons, and other legendary speed and exhibition shooters. First, a student has to be motivated to shoot quickly at a target. Second, a student must be instantly aware of a hit on the target in order to learn. From growing up hunting and then later trap and

Bill Rogers with Ken Hackathorn holding a Hackathorn Special, 1981.

Safariland's 013 competition holster, 2009

skeet shooting, I knew the easiest way to make a shooter quickly engage a target was to make the target appear and disappear quickly. But how do you make an efficient target system that can give the shooter immediate feedback?

The answer went back to my younger days of shooting at the county fair at the shooting gallery— a moving metal target that, when hit, would fall over and then reset before reappearing. With the help of a race car builder and driver, Terry Mock, who operated a shop next to mine, we designed and built a moving head-plate machine. It used a variable speed motor that operated an eccentric cam. The steel head plate, the size of a human head would move up and down on a slide. If knocked over in the up position, it would reset when it went down.

A steel cover, the height of the hood of a car, was built in front of the

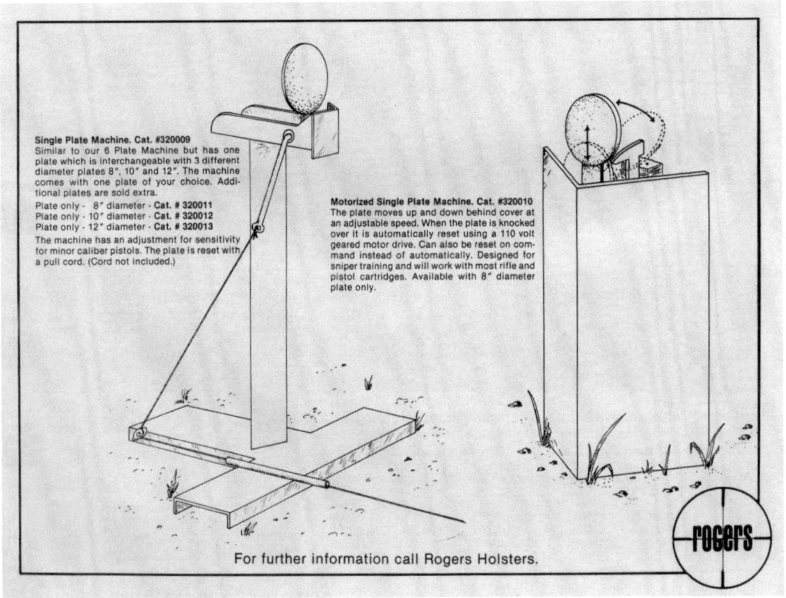

Steel reactive targets– Rogers Catalog 1982.

mechanism and the head would appear and disappear over the top of the shield. A set of micro switches would allow the machine to operate one cycle at a time. I adjusted the exposure time of the targets by changing the speed of the motor. I used a simple model airplane servo and transmitter to operate the target.

I leased a piece of property near Jacksonville Beach, Florida. It was owned by a local Fraternal Order of Police and had an existing backstop. I built cells on the range that were adjacent to each other and about 12 feet wide. In each cell I had two steel stationary targets and two moving head-plate machines. The first steel target in each cell was a moving head-plate machine, positioned about 7 yards from the shooter. The second was a stationary steel silhouette the same size as an official IPSC target, and was placed about 8 yards from the student, just slightly to the side of the moving head.

At 10 yards from the shooter and to the right of the silhouette stood another stationary steel target which was a "hostage" target. It was a body target the same size as an IPSC target but it had a head welded 12 inches behind and just to the left of the head of the front target. Ken Hackathorn had convinced me of the importance of having a critically accurate shot to which one must transition after engaging a close-range target.

At 15 yards was the final target, which was another moving head machine. I built six adjacent cells, each cell with the same array of four targets. I built walls, or baffles, that separated each cell so that a student shooting at the targets in one cell could not see any of the other targets. The moving head target in each cell was target number one, and they all worked on the same radio frequency. The last target in each cell was the other moving head. It was target number four and all six of them operated on the same frequency, but different from the frequency of target number one.

I could quickly set the speed control on the moving head targets to control the exposure time of the front and back targets. I used the front mover to start a drill and the back target to end the drill. Once I set up the drill, I could quickly run relays of students through that drill. After each student shot the drill, they would proceed forward and repaint the surface of all targets with white, water-based paint.

The drills required that the moving head be shot down before the end of the exercise. A low hit or ear shot would not usually knock over the mover, so the critically important skill of "follow through" was enforced. I called the system "Reaction Shooting" because the shooters were reacting to a surprise situation each drill and they had to perform in the time the targets were exposed. I called the targets "Reaction Targets" because, unlike cardboard or paper targets, they reacted by falling over.

I did not invent reaction shooting, I just coined the name. This was 1979 and no one else in the world had such a system. At first, I began to offer classes to individuals wanting to learn defensive pistol craft. I got students from many of the police departments I had sold holsters to. In time I got students from all over the country and Europe. "Reaction Shooting" as a teaching technique was off and running.

Contracts with the Special Forces

In 1980 the U.S. Navy SEALS were interested in me designing a special holster for them that could be used repeatedly in harsh environments. They sent down a young operator named Kevin Lundberg. Kevin grew up working as a commercial fisherman in Alaska and went by the nickname of Kodiak. He had taken on the assignment of getting the special holster developed. He lived at my house and went to work with me each day the first week. By the end of the week, we had a basic working prototype that we took into the ocean at Jacksonville Beach and swam with it.

When the weekend came around, I invited him to go to our range and shoot with my wife Christie and me. My wife and I were both part of the United States Practical Shooting Team, the U.S. affiliation of IPSC, and our only time to practice was on Saturday. Kevin told me he would like that very much. He said that his group shot a lot and that it was important for them to maintain their skill level. He said that he was one of the top shooters at his unit in Virginia Beach, but he didn't care for the new pistol they were being issued. He said that he preferred a custom built 1911 .45 or a Browning Hi-Power.

I opened my gun safe and told him to take his pick. He was like a poor kid in a candy store. He finally chose one of my .45's and the three of us headed to the range. As a warm up, Christie and I would always start with a common drill called the El Presidente in which you started with your back to three IPSC targets and upon the start signal, turned, shot two shots per target, reloaded and shot two more shots per target. We used a Pro-shot timer to record our times. On my range all my targets were steel. We just painted them white with water-based paint before each drill. We would start the drill at 25 yards and then move to 15 and finally 7 yards.

I painted the targets and then started the drill at 25 yards. In those days we could complete the drill with solid hits in less than 10 seconds at 25 yards and under 7 seconds at the 7 yard line. When I finished shooting, I repainted the targets and Christie prepared to do the drill. All the while, I noted that Kevin was very quiet.

Christie's cadence was not quite as fast as mine, but close and her hits were also solid. As I was repainting the targets, Kevin walked up to me and said, "I can't do that."

I asked him, "What part of it can't you do?"

He admitted that he could shoot that accurately, but nowhere near that fast.

I told him to just go ahead and shoot only as fast as he was comfortable. He shot very deliberately and although his hits were solid, his speed was agonizingly slow by our standards.

That night at dinner, Kevin was very quiet. At the end of the meal, he asked me if I could teach him how to shoot the way that Christie and I shot. I said that I could teach him everything he needed to know and do it in one week, if we worked a few hours each day after the holster project.

We used Sunday to set up one cell of my motorized targets at the range and we started shooting on Monday afternoon. At the end of the second week, we had accomplished two projects. We had developed a holster that for many years was the standard issue for the SEALs and I taught Kevin how to shoot head targets down in half a second.

A month later I received a call from Kevin's commanding officer, Richard Marcinko. He said that one of his boys was down at my range training and that he wanted me to teach all of his guys how to shoot the same way that Kevin had shot. I agreed.

That contact started a relationship with the Navy that continues to this day. Through this relationship, I have met many exceptional young men like Kevin who are dedicated to their unit and their country. Kevin was tragically lost on one of the first missions of the Granada invasion in November, 1983. Another SEAL student who originally came through my school in the early '80s, Francis "Dog" Faye, became instrumental in bringing units through our school in the early '90s. He has since retired from the Navy.

Not content with a ho-hum 8 to 5 job, he still leads the adventurous life as a Super Cub pilot and wildlife officer in Alaska. The challenges of flying a light aircraft in and around rough terrain is tough enough without throwing in ice, snow, high winds, mountain passes, and quickly deteriorating weather. I know there are many out there like me who envy his job. I'm doing my best to talk him into writing a book about his life and adventures. He could keep me entertained just with his flying stories.

During the late 1970 and early '80s, other special units of the military heard about my training and very soon all of my classes were booked with military units. I now had a problem dividing my time between the holster business, which was very demanding and stressful, and the shooting school which I loved. My class schedule became extremely busy.

I was committed to nearly 30 weeks a year with military Special Forces units. We taught through the summer and winter months. We booked classes during holidays and weekends. I can remember having a Navy SEAL platoon over for dinner one Thanksgiving evening. We were back to work at the range the next morning.

My military customers and I were concerned that my techniques would pass over to the "Dark Side". I signed non-disclosure agreements with the military and I kept everything about the school and my teaching techniques as low profile as I could. We did not advertise nor did we take civilians in the classes. We flew under the radar for many years.

During the first Gulf War, the Navy contracted with me to train new SEAL recruits how to shoot. I operated the range, which by now had been moved to Ellijay, Georgia, from the end of January, 1991 through the end of March with only a few days of rest. The weather during this period was brutal but we all survived. Some of those SEALS have since come back through the school and many of them state that their original basic firearms training provided for them at my school had served them well in combat.

For almost 20 years we taught exclusively the special units of our military and we avoided publicity. I would occasionally become envious of some of the other private shooting schools that continued to get press in magazines. In the end, the real measure of our success was how much business we had and what our customers thought about us, compared to the other schools. The standard sentiment was that if you qualified at even the basic level at the Rogers Shooting School, the other schools were just a cake walk.

Changing The FBI Shooting Program

In the spring of 1980, the FBI Firearms Training Unit (FTU) asked me if I would give a one day seminar on the type of training I was doing. I remembered the saying about not being an expert unless you were from out of town. Just seven years prior, my thoughts and ideas about firearms training were those of a meddling second office agent. In a short time I had gone from "chopped liver" to "expert."

Since my involvement with IPSC, I shot mainly .45 ACP 1911 Colt pistols and used the "Weaver" stance. The Bureau was still using revolvers, hip shooting and point-shoulder shooting with one hand. I knew if I showed up shooting a semi-auto pistol from a speed holster, my credibility would be toast. I shot pretty well with a revolver and could reliably shoot an 8.5 second El Presidente using speed loaders and my patented case called the "Six Pack."

I packed my trusty S&W Model 19 revolver, an inside-the-belt holster and my speed loaders. I was on a mission. I arrived at Quantico and was able to visit with my old friend Lester Limerick. I told him about my goal of changing the Bureau's style of instruction and he gave me the same advice that he had given me years before. He told me that the fundamental style of shooting and firearms instruction had not been changed in some 50 years and my attempt to bring such a radical departure from their time-tested regimen might alienate the Bureau.

By this time, the Bureau had become a major customer and, politically, this might not be a good business move. Lester was a wise man, but I chose to improve my average of not listening to him when it came to Bureau politics. I lectured for about four hours to the FTU instructors and went over most of the theories and concepts I'd developed, the same ideas that will be presented later in this book.

I finally came to the part of the lecture that was critical of hip shooting, point shooting and exclusive one-handed shooting for combat purposes. I stated that bringing a handgun to eye level and using two hands was an advantage in most real-life shootouts. During this era because of the influence of Jeff Cooper and IPSC competition I was teaching the "Weaver" stance, a two handed control of the handgun while using the sights of the weapon. My critical statements among the FBI FTU instructors were like calling a mother's baby ugly. I was preaching heresy and the situation almost got to name calling when I threw down the gauntlet. "Let's go to the range and I'll prove it," I said matter-of-factly.

At the range, the FTU picked their champion, Rollie Swanson. He was a great big man with large hands. When he fired his revolver there appeared to be no movement of the weapon in his hand. He was a superb hip and point-shoulder shooter.

Bill Rogers demonstrating "Weaver Technique at FBI Academy 1980.

Rollie Swanson demonstrating Bureau's hip shooting technique at the FBI Academy, 1980.

I handed out stop watches and explained the concept of Comstock scoring (score divided by time). To a man, they agreed that a scoring method that blended accuracy and speed seemed practical in order to test my techniques. I used the same target drills Ken Hackathorn had used on me several years before.

In the first few drills, Swanson was competitive, but he had not beaten me in time or points on any of the drills. When we got to the drill with two targets and the second one was a hostage situation, he was done. He hip-shot the first target, but when he transitioned to the hostage situation, he hesitated for a long time and then brought the revolver to eye level one-handed. The shots to the head of the target behind the hostage were very slow and deliberate.

When I shot the drill, there was no difference in the cadence of shots from the first to the second target, and I shot two shots in the head of the Tango target of the hostage situation that could be covered by a silver dollar. Things got real quite. I packed up my gear and went back to Florida.

Almost a year later I received a nice letter from the FBI FTU thanking me for my enlightening demonstration and stating that I had caused them to totally review their firearms training program that had been fundamentally unchanged since its inception. The letter stated that hip and point-shoulder shooting had been discontinued in favor of two-handed, eye-level shooting techniques. It is ironic how life goes. The odds against me bringing about a change in the shooting program of the FBI, had I remained an Agent, were probably a million to one.

I continued to teach at my range and actually traveled with my target system to several academies and military bases. I was hired to take my system to Hulburt Field which is part of Eglin Air Force Base. My contract was to train officers, from the rank of full colonel and above, to effectively carry a concealed handgun and defend themselves from an attack.

A half dozen Air Force small arms instructors (Red Caps) were assigned to me to carry out the instruction. Most of the officers did not know that I was a civilian contractor and there were many interesting situations that arose that would probably be a great topic for another book. One quick anecdote may be in order. I was amused to find on the first day of the class that each general was assigned an airman first class, to charge his Beretta 92 magazines. I had taught a lot of military units and had never seen this however I had never had any generals in

May 27, 1981

William H. Rogers
Alpha Plastics
P.O. Box 8028
Jacksonville, Fl. 32211

Dear Bill:

Although this is some time after you had visited us it truly gives us great pleasure in presenting this plaque to you. Your visit with us provided a tremendous incentive for us to take an in-depth look at the FBI's firearms training program. That in-depth look resulted in an evaluation which had never been done previously.

As you are probably aware, the FBI has adopted the Weaver stance and the results have been astounding. No longer do we have to spend those many hours and excessive amounts of ammunition in attempting to teach hip shooting.

Bo Johnson, Bob Dean, Tom Miller, and with the leadership and understanding of our Unit Chief Jim Weller, made a tremendous effort in the adoption of the Weaver stance. Many others in the Firearms Unit made contributions also and we are greatful to you for the time and effort you contributed to this end.

From the entire Firearms Training Unit,

Sincerely,

Gene Gilliland

Letter from the FBI Academy.

the classes. At the end of the first day of instruction I gathered all the students together and informed them that it was customary for shooters in my classes to police up their own brass. I quickly knelt down and began to pick up brass at the position where I had demonstrated all day. There was a long hesitation but finally one general bent over and began to pick up the brass. Instantly the others followed suit.

The classes ran for five straight days with 18 students per class. The contract ran for about six weeks. At the end of each class, I would hold a double elimination man vs. man shootout which would finally boil down to the last two shooters. In one class a two-star general had won all of his matches, including the final match. He looked around and said that he wanted to challenge one of the Red Cap instructors. I stepped up first, but he had watched me demo all week long and wanted no part of me.

He picked a master sergeant who was the senior man of the instructors. I knew the instructor was in real trouble. The general drew and shot down his targets before the sergeant could shoot down his first one. The general holstered his pistol and ordered the sergeant to try again and this time not to throw the match. I stepped in between the two and quietly advised the general that the sergeant was not throwing the match. I told him that neither the sergeant nor any of the other instructors had ever done this type of training and there would be no way that they could compete with him. He looked at me in disbelief. He thought that this type of training was provided by the Air Force to all the instructors and the "high speed" units that secured the base.

The sergeant advised the general that I was a civilian contractor and that no one in the Air Force, other than the high ranking officers in this program, had ever seen this type of training. The general's comment was quite colorful, but in a nutshell he felt the situation needed to be changed. I wound up selling several complete motorized range systems and re-writing much of the small arms training manual for the Air Force.

Rogers Pneumatic Reactive Target System

I sold several of the motorized target range systems to other military units and a few law enforcement academies before I began re-designing the system. The problem with the targets was that the bullet impact transferred through the steel and the micro switches would break. The other problem was that we were operating with 110 volt AC that was converted to DC at the motors. Protecting the high voltage wires from shorting or going to ground was a concern. It was a danger to the students as well as maintenance problem.

Again, with the help of Terry Mock, we designed a new target system that operated using compressed air. We used air cylinders in each target to operate the slides. The cylinders were actuated by electric air valves that used low voltage 12 volt DC. The new system worked very well and we were able to make every target in each cell operate with a moving slide.

We introduced a new target, our famous 3-Way target. It was a large steel wall that had three targets behind the wall. A target could come out over the wall or from each side of the wall. The side positions could be a low appearance, a foot off the ground, or a high position, about 4 feet off the ground. I still used radio controlled servo units to operate the targets. I had an analog timing circuit wired into each target. I had to set the exposure time on each target by turning a small dial. I kept all my drills in a note book and sometimes it would take me 15 minutes to set up a complicated drill. I still used the six identical cell arrangements on the range. The military operators referred to me as the "Wizard of Oz."

Around the fall of 1984, I was building a moving steel range at the Lively Law Enforcement Academy near Tallahassee, Florida. (It is now known as the Pat Thomas Academy.) Two young men were also there installing a turning paper target range. Their targets operated with compressed air also, but they used a computer to operate the timing of the targets. They had a small box that interfaced with the computer. Wires ran from the control box to the targets and they were buried under ground. The software was fairly easy to learn even though it was long before any Windows type program was available.

The two young men were fresh out of school and did not know much about shooting, but they were smart and they had a control system that I desperately needed. Addison Sovigne and Kyle Bateman were from Provo, Utah and they had just started a company called Action Targets. I desperately wanted their software program and they became interested in my pop-up target system. Before our respective installations at that range were completed, we had worked a deal.

They would license me to use and sell their software/hardware system with my steel moving targets if I would license them to manufacture and sell my target array. We could compete head on if an agency requested a bid for the complete system. I was never really interested in selling target systems; I was interested in promoting my theories and techniques of teaching. For me, this was a win, win situation.

Within a few months of getting one of Action Targets' "Smart Range" controllers, the lease on my range expired. The city of Jacksonville Beach did not want a shooting range since a huge developer wanted to build million-dollar homes nearby. The potential tax revenue from those homes was the final nail in the coffin for the range. I was out of the shooting school business.

To obtain permits to build a new shooting range in Florida was near impossible. The land is flat and to build berms tall enough to stop bullets is cost-prohibitive. I began to ask people I knew in the shooting industry if they knew of any range for sale or lease.

One of those people was Art Hill, a friend from Ellijay, Georgia. He had grown up shooting most of his life. After a stint in the Army he had worked for many years as a salesman and professional shooter with Winchester. I believe he then worked for Mossberg, but when I first met him he was in charge of sales for the Don Hume Holster Company. He was a respected competitor. I considered myself as a pretty good salesman, but I was no Art Hill. I believe he could sell anything, but his expertise was the firearms industry. I do not think Art ever forgot a name and he knew practically everybody that shot or bought shooting supplies. He knew firearms. He was a shooter and collector. He was like a walking, talking reference library when it came to shooting equipment. He was the best salesman I ever met and his wife Bess was the best cook I ever met. We were friends from the beginning, but we became much closer when he left Hume and went to work for Browning.

In 1984 Art called me and said that he was planning to move from Oklahoma back to his original home of Ellijay. He was going to build a home there and retire. He said that a piece of property was sold out of his family and was back up for sale. His property surrounded this piece that was up for sale and he was interested in having a good neighbor. He said the property was a flat section of land located in a valley with mountains all around. I traveled to Ellijay and immediately after seeing the property, I bought it. It took me about six months to build the range with six shooting cells with baffles and a front facade. Art Hill supervised the construction of the skeet and trap ranges. I also built a 150 yard reactive steel rifle range. The reactive targets were of the new design and were now operated by Action Targets' magic computerized controller. With a keystroke, I could change the whole range to a new drill. It was wonderful. I was back in the shooting school business.

The Safariland Purchase

Neale Perkins, the owner of Safariland Ltd, had started a holster business in the early 1960s with a partner, John Bianchi. Shortly afterward the two went their separate ways and the Bianchi and Safariland companies became very competitive against each other. Both companies used traditional leather in their products and relied on handcrafted quality. Both men were not only creative in product design, but also they were innovative in marketing their products.

In 1983 Neale had witnessed me destroying one of his all leather duty holsters in a Level 1 security test at one of the trade shows. He was interested in my SSII and SSIII holsters, but more importantly he recognized that my Thermo-laminate process was the way of the future. He asked me to design a safety holster using my process and to teach Safariland how to manufacture it. It was a revolver holster, model 275. It was a front opening holster that worked like our Boss holster but did not have the same securing strap mechanism. Neale also wanted to market my new speed loader case called the 6-Pack. I was to be paid a simple royalty based on the sales of the two products.

Neale believed that we had two separate markets. My holster sales were strong in the southeast and his company was strong in the west. He was correct. After our agreement, he began manufacturing and selling the model 275 that was similar to one of my models, yet both of our sales continued to grow. The Safariland royalty grew to almost equal my salary from the holster company.

A year later, Safariland had been very successful in marketing the two products. Neale realized the potential of my process and designs and wanted to grow his business with my technology. He called and said he wanted to buy my holster company, and have me agree to a 20 year consulting agreement. I would still design products, but Safariland would manufacture and market them. At the time I had 42 employees. I had the holster business, an ammunition business, a bullet manufacturing business, a gun parts business, a target business, and a booming shooting school business. A fork in the road appeared. The decision I made would definitely alter the direction of my life.

There was a whole lot going on and I was about to go nuts. With Neale's offer I believed another life line was being thrown to me and I reached out for it. Safariland purchased the Rogers Holster Company, but they did not want any of the other businesses. I sold the gun parts business to Bill Wilson and the bullet and ammunition business to an employee and friend, Cyril "Rosie" Rosel.

I formed a research and consulting company to design products for Safariland and in that company I included the target business and the shooting school. I could now devote more time to testing my theories about teaching firearms skills without feeling guilty about neglecting the other businesses. I also could use the school as a test bed for future firearms related products.

Since the sale of the Rogers Holster Company in 1985, I have been involved in the development and manufacture of numerous firearms products and have been awarded over 30 patents. Even though I sold the Rogers Holster Company to Safariland in 1985, I have continued to design and be involved with the manufacture of holsters and other equipment related to the shooting industry. That business has been highly successful by any standard, but I did not accomplish it alone. I have some great people who work with me. These include very gifted people like Norman "Buzzy" Clifton who is now a partner; Greg Gossett, our pattern maker and forming expert; and several other people like Teri James, and Cathy Powell who have worked with me for years and are responsible for taking ideas and transforming them into working products. We continue today as Prezine LLC, with over 20 employees to produce designs and products that are marketed by Safariland and others in the firearms industry.

My shooting school has become famous for teaching "leading edge" shooting techniques and is known by most high-speed military units as "The School" to attend. Since the sale of the holster business, the school has been my primary focus, so it's time to share with you some of what I've learned about shooting techniques for the last half century.

How the Mind Works

I do not pretend to be a behavioral scientist or a psychologist, nor have I had any formal education in biomechanics or neurophysiology. However, over the years I have done considerable study of these subjects. Much of what is written in the academic journals does not apply to firearms training. What I am writing about here on the subjects of human biomechanics and how the human mind affects our fine and gross motor skills are my own beliefs, based on observations of results to my own experiments.

The mind can be generally divided in to two sections, the conscious and subconscious. The conscious mind can listen and follow verbal directions. It can remember things previously read. It can recall ideas and techniques formally learned. It can use logic, formulate theories, and use deduction. The subconscious mind, on the other hand, can only recall what it has been taught through constant repetition. The two parts of the mind can operate independently and normally do.

On the way home from work, you may find your conscious mind thinking about problems at work or plans for the weekend, while the subconscious mind is driving your vehicle. Some people call it driving on "auto pilot." The subconscious mind is maintaining proper speed, obeying traffic lights, keeping a safe distance away from the vehicle in front and taking any evasive action in order to avoid an accident. The subconscious is relying totally on past repetitions of experience to manage the numerous skills necessary to drive a car.

If you wish to teach the subconscious how to respond correctly to an action, you must teach it by correct repetition. For years we have had heard that, "Practice makes perfect," but an astute person who really understood the learning process made it even better with the observation that, "Perfect practice makes perfect."

To teach someone to drive a car through an obstacle course at 100 mph, you would not limit their speed to only 35 mph in training. To teach someone how to fight, you would not require them to "pull" their punches in training. This seems obvious in almost all training that requires quick eye hand coordination... except conventional firearms training.

Historically, police academies and military agencies have taught slow, methodical shooting to their students. Most federal law enforcement agencies teach their students to hit a man-sized target with one shot in 1.5 seconds at 10 yards, starting with the handgun out and extended. After weeks of such training, they somehow believe that in a real gun battle their students will be able to shoot much faster and still hit their adversary. Later on in this book, I will explain why these agencies have chosen this counterproductive training and why they must change their methods.

For the remainder of your life remember this truth: To learn a correct, conditioned response to a quick action, you must learn that response through correct repetition at the quickest possible speed. In one week my students are trained to hit a head-sized target at 10 yards in half a second.

Condition White

"Condition White" is when there is a true separation between the conscious mind and the subconscious, such as with the driving example just mentioned. Most accidents occur while the mind is in this condition. The conscious mind can be deeply involved in some analytical thought process while the subconscious is on "auto pilot." Under normal circumstances, if the subconscious is trained properly, it can operate safely without much oversight by the conscious mind. However, some of the conditioned responses we have acquired through life can create dangerous situations under certain scenarios.

Throughout life we have trained ourselves to catch things that are rolling off a table or to stop something from falling that has been tipped. But this automatic reflex to catch something from falling has proven to be fatal when, for instance, medical researchers in a lab have tried catching a dropped syringe with a contaminated needle tip and have pricked themselves. Today contaminated needles have an automatic seal that protects examiners from such accidents. No matter how acutely aware these lab technicians were that the needles were infectious with HIV or other contaminants, their subconscious reflex to catch a falling object reacted faster than their conscious mind could counter.

Occasionally, something interrupts our mental system briefly and a sequence is left out. The subconscious continues to operate just as it has been trained, not realizing that a critical sequence has been abandoned. This is why even the most highly trained aircraft pilots rely on a check list. Quite a few years ago, an acquaintance of mine was mowing the grass on a riding mower that had a grass bagging attachment. He had had an altercation with his teenage son that morning and his conscious mind was deep in thought about that problem. His normal procedure was to shut down the mower when the grass bag was filled. He would detach the bag and dump it.

Upon returning to the mower, he would clear the clogged grass from the port, reinstall the bag, and restart the mower. This morning, however, his subconscious missed one slight detail and failed to shut down the mower. He continued to follow out the sequences even though the engine was running at full power, vibrating, blowing out hot exhaust gases, and making plenty of noise. When he went to clear the clogged port, he lost his left hand. To prevent this type of accident, present day mowers have a failsafe switch that shuts down the engine and blade as soon as weight is removed from the seat.

Many shooting accidents have a similar root cause. Shooters have gone through a cleaning or dry fire operation for many years until everything is habit. Then, for an instant, the mind fails to follow procedure and an accidental shot is fired. If the subconscious mind has not been trained to never point the muzzle of a firearm at anything it does not intend to harm, then the accidental shot can be a fatal one.

When I was an Agent in Chicago many years ago, an armored car guard accidentally shot and killed a young man on the street. He had a habit of passing time inside the back of the truck when it was parked by unloading his revolver and dry firing at pedestrians across the street through one of the small portals. Instead of using the ejector rod, he would simply open the cylinder and let gravity drop the cartridges in his hand. One day only five shells dropped in his hand and he did not notice that the sixth round was still in the cylinder.

Firearms, like many other pieces of equipment, can be very dangerous if the subconscious is not properly trained. However, sometimes this is not enough. We should maintain some conscious oversight anytime we are dealing with a piece of equipment that, if mishandled, could cause injury or death.

Condition Yellow

"Condition Yellow" is that condition in which the conscious mind is constantly alert and aware of the possible dangers that are present. Driving home from work, your conscious mind needs to be able to immediately identify a potential danger such as the beginning of light rain, ice, or bad lighting conditions. Your conscious mind needs to be aware of suspicious activities of others around you. It needs to be able to quickly identify anomalies.

If your neighbor is on vacation, there should not be a panel van parked outside the garage. Beware of a guy in a parked car outside the 7-11 with the motor running and the car is facing outward. We must be aware of body language and acts of aggression towards us by others. The first act of aggression in all animals is "eye to eye" contact. Some ill-trained individuals notice this act of aggression and even though they become uncomfortable, they continue along a predetermined course of action until it is too late to have a tactical advantage.

Someone once said that if you are ever involved in a fair fight, it's because you don't understand the importance of tactics. Condition Yellow is the condition we need to be in when we are driving, running a chain saw, or working with any dangerous piece of equipment, including a firearm.

Condition Orange

"Condition Orange" is a mental state that is triggered by a specific challenge. Many believe that the challenge must be associated with a threat of death or injury, but this is not true. Simply the fear of losing is enough to trigger the mental state and associated levels of anxiety. I myself have been deep in Condition Orange, triggered by a difficult match like the Moving Target Event at the NRA Action Shooting National Championship (Bianchi Cup) shoot. For many years I have witnessed motivated and highly trained Special Forces individuals experience the condition during a test at my range just because of the fear of failing in the presence of their peers. When the challenge presents itself, psychological and physiological changes take place immediately.

Within 10 seconds or less, the body undergoes some significant changes. Heartbeat is increased as the body prepares for possible battle. Pain inhibitors began streaming through the blood system. We develop an upper body tremor. Our voice pitch is elevated. Our hands seem cold and clammy. We have a knot in our stomach and our mouth is dry. We have an immediate loss of appetite. The body begins to eliminate certain body waste and in a short time we begin to exude body odors and we need to urinate. As long as the challenge continues, the body remains in this elevated state. Restful sleep is difficult. People tend to doze for 45 minute intervals and awaken startled. In many cases the emotional stress causes diarrhea.

As the challenge becomes imminent, it is common for people and other animals to begin shallow breathing or even to repress breathing altogether. This shallow breathing may have helped our caveman forefathers hide from attack or execute a successful ambush, but it also depletes oxygen in our system and makes fine motor skills difficult. This interrupted breathing just prior to an engagement did not create much of a disadvantage when our only weapon was a club, but it is very detrimental to controlling the trigger of a firearm. For years I have taught my students that when a challenge was imminent, they should begin to force themselves to breathe deeply and even to hyperventilate.

The most serious concern about Condition Orange is the psychological changes that take place in humans. Doubt— which in turn triggers levels of anxiety— becomes a debilitating enemy. Improperly trained people fall into what I call the "Wait-And-See" syndrome. Their mind does not want to deal with the possibility of failure, so in order to avoid such a thought it simply says, "Things will be alright.We'll just wait and see." This mental aberration is responsible for the death of a large percentage of those lost in combat.

The "Wait-And-See" syndrome provides mental comfort to the situation and coaxes our subconscious into a false sense of security, but it doesn't allow for the conscious mind to deal with the actual reality and to continue planning for survival. In this condition, people continue to execute a plan that is hours or even days old even though critical elements have changed.

A woman, who might have become uncomfortable by a stalking incident in a grocery store, leaves the store with her groceries in hand and proceeds directly to her vehicle, even when the stalker is nearby. Police officers will continue to advance into an unknown situation without stopping to question the circumstances, until the situation becomes un-survivable. Military operators will continue to press on during a mission gone badly wrong until they are lost.

In conveying these sorts of scenarios to students, I used to describe situations that I was personally aware of or involved in, but now I tell my students to simply watch the movie "Blackhawk Down." This movie documents a series of scenarios where the "Wait-And-See" syndrome played an important role in the tragic loss of a number of soldiers.

For years I have warned my students that the most meticulously scripted missions, raids, and arrests rarely go as planned. Subjects never seem to look like the photo you have. Communications almost always have problems and plans that are based around closely timed events seldom come off without a hitch. If the helicopter that brought you and your team into a hot zone is shot down, then you should not count on another one to extract you anytime soon.

I tell my students that they must rely on their own judgment and skills. The second reliance is reserved for a trusted partner, then the squad. I tell them not to count on anything past the squad level.

What is the alternative to the "Wait-And-See" syndrome? The answer is what I call the "What If?" mind set. "What If" our deployment helicopter is shot down on the way into a mission that is planned to take only a few minutes to complete? Do we have an alternate escape plan, maps, GPS unit, extra water and ammo, local currency to bribe non-combative local inhabitants, and night vision equipment for an extended battle?

"What If" a parachute drop is planned to happen just before sunset and the drop plane encounters heavy head winds. Do we have a plan to rendezvous in the dark? Does everyone know the recognition signal and have chem lights to form up on?

Once you begin to practice the "What If" mind set and count on Murphy's Laws to rule the mission, you will find that you are more confident and are prepared when things begin to go badly wrong.

If you don't get anything else of value from my book, I hope you remember the following advice: You may be alone or with someone else that you need to protect. You may be walking in a parking lot outside of a movie theater or down a lonely street. You notice a stranger who is heading on a path that will intercept yours. Your heart begins to beat harder. You have a knot in your stomach and your hands have an uncontrollable shake. You begin to shallow breath. Stop! Do not continue! Do not press forward in the same direction and "wait and see" what happens. Remember this book! Take a few deep breaths and state to yourself, "What if this guy intends to hurt or kill me?" Now determine your objective. Then quickly list your assets and your alternatives to the solution. Make a plan and initiate it, with the understanding that objectives can change in a few seconds and if they do, you must react to those changes.

This same procedure should be used by the police officer who has received a call to respond to shots fired and also to the military operator on a dangerous mission. Define the objective. Then list assets and alternative plans to accomplish the objective. Make a plan and stick to it until the objective changes. Without this mind set you will likely continue in the same original direction that may prove to be fatal.

Secondly, prepare yourself in advance of a confrontation. I recommend that in this day and age that every family have a well-rehearsed plan to deal with certain emergencies. Every member of the family should know his or her role in dealing with a fire evacuation. They should know and practice different evacuation routes, depending on the location of the fire. They need to know immediately what they consider precious to grab and escape with. At 4:00 a.m. in the morning with a fire in the house, it's not the time for a child to try and sort out what doll or blanket is important.

I used to walk into my children's bedroom and announce a 30 second fire drill. They had 30 seconds to pick what stayed and what they could escape with. I would then tell them where the imaginary fire was and let them quickly tell me how they would escape.

Home invasion and kidnapping are other situations that should be considered and discussed. Some believe that this type of training leads to paranoia. I believe it teaches important skills that can save lives. Every member of the family should know his or her responsibilities and be cross-trained to react if one of the other family members is unable to act. They should all know the "What If" game and be able to format a plan under different given variables.

Families should have a "lost comms" plan. There could be a natural or man-made disaster that wipes out cell phones and land lines. A set plan on where and when to meet, or other means of communication or a pre-arranged plan, could prove to be life saving. Teaching this type of mental conditioning to your children could save their lives many years after they are no longer your responsibility.

If you are in the military or part of a rapid response team with a law enforcement agency, I recommend having what I call a "go to war bag."

In this day and age, it may be important even for civilians to have a "go bag" to rely on to protect themselves and family in case of a disaster. If you have a favorite knife that holds an edge, don't wear it out, put it in the bag. If you have any piece of personal gear that you find works really well, then keep that gear pristine and put it in the bag. That goes for boots, socks, knee pads, holster, pistol, magazines, gas mask, load-bearing or armored vests, Leatherman tools and anything that you would want in an emergency.

The bag should have a small chemical or membrane water purifier and some general and specific antibiotics and other emergency medicines. You should have a couple of good quality hand held radios, a hand-held GPS, and a supply of batteries. You should have some cash, including gold in small coin denominations. When the time comes, you can grab that bag and have confidence in everything that's inside. It can be mentally very comforting at a time when you need your wits about you.

Condition Red

"Condition Red" is triggered when the ship hits the sand. When the bullets are impacting around you or the fists are flying and you are in the heat of battle, you will undergo greater changes than Condition Orange. Again the changes will take place in less than 10 seconds from start of the battle, but they do not happen instantly like some people believe.

The heart beat will almost double-speed from a rested condition. The body has an uncontrollable quiver. Don't worry about the skip breathing problem associated with Condition Orange. You will be breathing hard and barely able to catch your breath even though you have not exerted yourself. Everything will seem to be going in slow motion, a phenomenon known as tachypsychia. You will experience tunnel vision. That is, you will be so focused on what your perception of the threat is that you may not see other, more obvious dangers.

You will also experience audio exclusion. You may not hear directions or warnings shouted at you. Many gunfight participants report that they never heard the gunfire. You will have super strength and you are not likely to feel much pain unless you anticipate the injury.

Mentally you will be much like in Condition White, with a true separation of the conscious and the subconscious. The logic and planning part of the conscious mind simply doesn't work. You're not able to mentally solve the simplest of puzzles. The conscious mind will be overwhelmed with multiple thoughts while the subconscious will do only that which it has been taught— through correct repetition— and it will do it only as fast as it has practiced. This final concept is the basis for how we train at the Rogers Shooting School.

Precision Shooting Skills

I divide shooting skills into two major categories. The first category is what I call "precision shooting". Simply stated, a precision shot is a shot fired in the shooter's own allotted time. The epitome of a precision shot is the term commonly referred to as a "surprise break." This term is normally understood to mean that the shooter steadies the firearm and begins to press or squeeze the trigger until the sear releases the hammer, causing the weapon to fire before that firing is precisely anticipated.

There are necessary elements to a precision shot before the trigger press action is initiated. Everything must be stabilized. First the target must be stabilized. It can be moving but if it is, the speed and direction must be predictable. Second, the shooter must be stabilized. Finally, the firearm must be guided by some precise sighting system while the movement or wobble of the firearm is reduced so that the precise sighting device remains well defined and aligned near the point of the intended impact of the bullet. We many times refer to this as a perfect sight picture.

During this refinement of the alignment of the firearm, the controlling of one's breath is necessary. We are of course assuming that the conscious mind has already given the order to fire the shot when all is ready. When all is ready the mind initiates a press-press-press motion of the trigger until the weapon fires. When the shot finally breaks, it's a "surprise" to the shooter because his compression of the trigger has been isolated from his subconscious mind.

The elements of precision shooting are sometimes described in the most basic terms as "sight alignment and trigger control." One of the necessary ingredients for a successful precision shot is a good trigger. When a "good" trigger is operated, the subconscious mind does not exactly know when the weapon will fire. Most skilled precision shooters opt for a very light trigger pull, usually less than 3 pounds. Some like the trigger action like that of a well set-up 1911 pistol. We describe the action like bending a glass rod until it snaps. Some like a mushy trigger like compressing a sponge and then the weapon fires. The end result is that we are trying to achieve that surprise break.

About the fastest that a skilled shooter can fire a precision shot is around 1.25 seconds. Shooting sports that demand precision such as bull's eye, the various Olympic disciplines such as Free Pistol, and other shooting sports like metallic silhouette, PPC, and bench rest allow much more time than 1.25 seconds.

To test this theory, put a one inch dot on a piece of cardboard at 10 yards away. Use a shot timer to time six shots. Trying to hit the dot each shot as fast as you can achieve a surprise break. Look at your times. They will rarely be less than 1.25 seconds per shot.

Precision shots are difficult if not impossible to perform under stressful conditions such as Condition Red because necessary stabilization cannot be achieved. Is precision shooting a necessary skill in real life? Absolutely. A sniper relies on the fundamentals of precision shooting. A hunter, 100 yards or more from his prey, must employee the same fundamentals. A shooter just trying to zero his firearm must rely on precision skills. Precision skills are very important and a skilled shooter must have those skills.

Most instructors believe that precision shooting skills are the basic fundamentals to all shooting and that they should be taught first. I not only do not agree, but also I go so far as to assert that precision shooting, if taught first, is very counterproductive. If it is the only form of instruction given to people, who must defend themselves with a firearm, it can prove to be very dangerous.

Unfortunately, I am one of the few instructors who feel this way and I do not know of any other academy that teaches basic firearms the way I do. You may disagree with me at this point of the book, but please keep an open mind and hear me out.

Reactive Shooting

Simply stated, a reactive shot is fired not in the shooter's own time, but in the time that the target is available to the shooter. The best example to a reactive shot is a bird hunter downing a fast-moving dove that is taking evasive action over a dove field. For those of you reading this book that are not skilled at shooting live birds, skeet, trap, or sporting clays, I will explain.

Unlike precision shooting, nothing is stabilized before the reactive shot takes place. In precision shooting, we wait until the wobble of the sight picture is minimized before we start the press action of the trigger. In reactive shooting, we cannot take the time to reduce the wobble of the weapon before pulling the trigger. We drive the sight and associated weapon toward the target. Our subconscious determines a solution to the problem of hitting the target based on prior experience. When that solution is recognized, the weapon is instantly fired.

Although the weapon is instantly fired when the mind recognizes the solution, the mind has initiated the trigger pull well before the weapon is aligned. This situation is much like a baseball batter who must start his swing well before the ball is over the plate. I call finding this firing solution "reaching the green light."

The subconscious needs only enough information to solve the problem. At close distances it may only need the alignment of the top of the slide of the pistol. A more difficult shot may require a more refined alignment of the firearm's sights. Your mind will know exactly what alignment and how refined that alignment must be, just like your mind knows what lead it needs to hit a quail moving at 40 miles an hour, climbing as it flies away from you at a right angle. It, however, can only know this "green light" moment because of prior training.

Unlike precision shooting, we do not have the time to control our breathing. There is no such thing as a "perfect sight picture." We do not press–press-press the trigger and there is no such thing as a surprise break. Our subconscious mind knows within a few milliseconds of when the shot will fire because it is perfectly timing the shot. Almost all shots become moving target shots even though the target may be stationary.

Unlike a typical precision shot that requires the wobble to be reduced to a certain degree, the mind simply times the shot to happen the instant that the firearm is aligned. Triggers do not need to be light, and in fact, should not be below 3 pounds. Triggers must, however, be reliable and must release consistently under the same exerted pressure. Because nothing is stabilized prior to the shot, we are capable of making a reactive shot while in Condition Red, breathing hard, or moving.

A precision shot usually takes 1.25 to 1.5 seconds to hit a humanoid target at 10 yards, starting with the handgun out and extended generally toward the target. That same shot fired as a reactive shot should take half a second.

How fast and how accurate can we execute a reactive shot with a firearm? This answer relies on the type of instruction the shooter is given and also on the physical and mental makeup of the student. However, the limit is controlled by human reaction and response times. How does a shooter trained in reactive shooting transition to a precision shot when greater accuracy is required? It is intuitive.

The mind learns quickly that in order to hit a very small target or one at a greater distance, the sights must be refined and the movement of the firearm must be steadied. However, the person who is taught reactive shooting skills rarely takes more than 1.25 seconds to break a shot with a high degree of accuracy. In our next chapter we will talk about how to begin training ourselves to make an accurate reactive shot.

Training For A Reactive Shot

Remember that a reactive shot is not shooting in our own time, but in the time the target is exposed to us. Recall my earlier admonition, "To learn a correct conditioned response to a quick action, you must learn that response through correct repetition at the quickest possible speed."

We commonly use the term "reaction time" to describe quick hand-eye reactions; however, for our discussion here "response time" is a more realistic term to use. Response time is the sum of "reaction time" and the associated "movement time" necessary to complete the task. This subject matter has been studied for years and the literature is filled with data from experiments. With the use of our present day electronic shot timers, it is relatively easy to do our own tests to determine what is possible.

First, set the shot timer to random start. Press the start button and upon hearing the start signal, simply tap the unit near the impact sensor with your finger. The resulting concussion will register the time from the signal to the impact, or your response time. With a little practice you should be able to do this drill around .25 of a second. We now know that it takes about .25 of a second to accomplish a very simple response to a specific drill.

If we add a second identical action to automatically follow the first action, such as tapping the timer twice each time we hear the signal, with the same finger, we will find that the first tap is still about .25 of a second but the second is actually slightly faster. It usually is timed around .20 of a second. Most neurologists believe this shorter time is because the exact action being repeated is following an electrical path of neurons that are still warm from the previous event.

If, however, we add a second, but different, action to follow the first, in immediate succession, such as tapping the timer with one finger followed by tapping a second finger of the same hand, we find that the total time closely represents the sum of two response times.

Most actions in shooting require at least two response times, or a half second. To simply lift a handgun to eye level from a downward extended position and then stop it to aim at a finite point, requires two response times. One reaction time is allocated for the shooter to recognize a start stimulus, and one movement time is allocated to drive the weapon toward the intended spot. A second reaction time is required to recognize that the weapon is approaching the intended spot and a second movement time is required to stop the weapon at the predetermined spot. In order to fire the weapon in this half second time limit, the human body must learn to multitask and pull the trigger as it lifts the weapon to the point of alignment.

Theoretically, a shooter could respond to a stimulus, lift the weapon to eye level and fire two shots (a double tap), hitting a finite spot with both shots in less than .75 seconds. In order to do this we must initiate the trigger pull as we drive the firearm toward the intended mark. If we wait to align the firearm before our mind is given the go ahead to fire the shot, we must at a minimum add another response time. Now that we know what is possible, let's put our response time knowledge to the test. Before we do, however, I need you to read the next chapter on dry fire practice.

Dry Fire Practice

Dry fire is an extremely important learning tool; however, it poses serious dangers if done improperly. Remember you are training the subconscious mind. The subconscious does not know logic, tactics, theories, deduction, or analysis. It only knows what it's been programmed through consistent repetition. Remember my friend with the lawn mower.

People who become careless with a firearm while dry firing are actually teaching their subconscious mind very dangerous habits. If you become lackadaisical about picking up a firearm and working the action without first checking that it is unloaded— even though you "know" it's unloaded— you will eventually have a negligent or accidental discharge. We must treat the dry fire training as if the firearm is loaded with live ammo.

First, choose a place in your home that has a wall that will stop a fired pistol cartridge. Brick, block, or concrete walls should be chosen, not sheetrock. If there is no exterior wall in your home that will stop a pistol bullet, you will need to construct something and put it in place. The room you have chosen will be the only room where you will ever dry fire. There will be no live ammunition in that room and you should put a small sign outside the opening of that room that warns you and anyone else to unload any firearm before entering.

Place a table outside the room so that you can leave any charged magazines, speed loaders, or live ammo before entering that room. This room and the designated wall or constructed bullet trap area will be the only place in your home where you will dry fire. If you should pull the trigger of your firearm any place else in the house, you should expect to hear a loud noise and a bullet should exit the barrel.

You should mount your target or "spots" on your safety wall. Vary the height and size of the targets to represent close and distant targets. There are several good dry fire programs that are available so it's wise to have access to a CD or DVD player in the room. You should never indulge in alcohol or any other mind or reflex altering chemicals before or during your dry fire session. You should operate in the room just as you would on a commercial range facility, treating the safety wall as the "down range" area.

Even as careful as you may be, there is still a chance that you will someday have an accidental discharge in the dry fire room. If you've followed the rules, you will not have injured anyone. You can also use this room to clean your firearm, but that's not mandatory. You, of course, will be sure that your weapon is unloaded before starting to clean your firearm no matter where you choose to clean it. If it is not in the dry fire room, you will not start dry firing the firearm after you clean it. Now we can proceed on with our learning process.

Stance

Handgun shooting techniques have evolved over the last 150 years but they have changed dramatically in the last 40. Up until the 1970s most handgun instruction and shooting was done with one hand. Hip shooting and point-shoulder techniques were developed for combat shooting in the 1920s and were popular into the late 1960s. Bull's eye competition, a one-handed shooting discipline with an emphasis on slow, deliberate sighted fire was popular in the 1950s. Formalized PPC competition shooting in the '60s brought about the use of both hands and the adoption of a true isosceles stance.

The Isosceles is a position in which the shooter stands erect with both knees straight and with both feet parallel and abeam each other, separated about the width of one's shoulders. Both arms are fully extended to form an isosceles triangle with the chest, and the handgun is held with both hands. The body and the head are kept straight in line and the handgun is raised to eye level. The balance of the shooter is pretty much down the centerline of the body.

The actual grip on a handgun varied. Some chose to cup the bottom of the grip with the support hand while others gripped and supported the wrist and shooting hand with the support hand. Still others let the fingers of the support hand wrap around the shooting hand with the support thumb pressing tightly on the shooting hand between the thumb and forefinger knuckles. Even though the isosceles position dominated PPC competition shooting, it was considered by many not to be a true combat position. It was a stable shooting position for shooting the very light loads used in PPC shooting but because of the straight knees and erect posture, it did not work well for rapid firing of major caliber loads. Also, because the feet of the shooter were parallel and the toes were on the same line, the shooter was immobile. The shooter would have to take a half step before being able to move forward or backwards.

In the early 1960s a group of shooters formed a club in southern California, known as the Southwest Combat Pistol League that conducted what they called "leather slap" or quick-draw shooting matches. These matches eventually evolved into a sport now known as International Practical Shooting Confederation or IPSC. A stance known as the "Weaver," named after Jack Weaver, a sheriffs' deputy, began to dominate the local matches.

The leather slap events were designed to test combat handgun shooting skills. Major caliber pistol loads, 9mm and above, were required for competition and a unique scoring of the event, named after another SWPL member, Walt Comstock, was used. As noted earlier, Comstock scoring (or hits divided by time) produced a winning factor that gave an equal importance to speed and accuracy.

History is unclear as to whether Weaver actually used the one bent elbow, isometric "push-pull" technique, so well described and promoted by the late Col. Jeff Cooper. Weaver was once quoted as saying that, "What I remember was that I used both hands, brought the handgun to eye level and I used my sights."

Regardless, Cooper and others believed that the Weaver technique was the best way to control true defensive handguns with real combat loads. Besides the bladed body stance and bent support elbow, Cooper promoted a support hand grip that placed the forefinger in front of the trigger guard of the pistol. This hand position was supposed to enhance the "pull back" of the pistol to help stabilize it during recoil. This technique became so dominate that most of the firearms companies changed their designs to include a square front trigger guard, or even a hook, with some type of checkering. Cooper was an exceptional writer and lecturer and through his leadership, formed an international shooting confederation that tested combat shooting skills under a competitive sports forum internationally.

By the late 1970s, the Weaver stance and associated grip were considered the cutting edge technique for "real combat handgun shooting." The bladed stance with the radically bent support elbow became the overwhelming dominate position used in combat shooting all over the world. It is still taught today by many of the less progressive instructors in the industry.

In the early 1980s two young shooters from Arizona began to win some IPSC matches around the country. Brian Enos and Rob Leatham had competed in local "combat" matches sponsored by the Cactus Combat Match League in Phoenix, Arizona, but much of their training was competing against each other with drills that they had designed. They were essentially self-taught and had not been influenced by the Weaver technique which, at this time, was considered the standard among IPSC competitors.

Their stance was a modified version of the Isosceles. Instead of standing totally erect, they bent forward at the waist. Their backs made an arch and their heads tilted slightly forward. Their knees were bent and their left foot was slightly in front of their right foot. They were both right-handed shooters but both arms were extended equally and both hands adapted to the grip of the handgun so as to contact as much of the surface of the handgun grip as possible. Neither used their support forefinger on the front of the trigger guard, but allowed it to continue to wrap around the shooting hand to increase pressure on the grip of the pistol.

The end result was that much of their weight was forward of the centerline of their body. Instead of standing erect and raising the handgun to eye level, they arched their backs forward, extended their arms to a comfortable position, and lowered their heads to a position to look through the sights of the handgun. Their shooting technique stood out like a sore thumb among the Weaver aficionados, but they were winning matches against many of us who had a great deal more experience.

Was it possible that their technique was better than the famed Weaver position? Just the thought was considered heresy. Historically, the new technique should have been called the Enos-Leatham, or Leatham-Enos, because they promoted that style by beating us in matches. However, the entire industry had bought off on the Weaver style and many egos could not stand the change.

I have always believed that history is not determined by who wins or loses a battle, but who is allowed to write the history books. Many of us quietly began to test the new technique. Within a few days of practice, it was obvious that the Leatham-Enos technique was superior to the Weaver. Shooters who had used the Weaver technique for years had changed overnight to the new style of shooting.

Cooper was demoralized and vowed to design more "realistic" matches that would once and for all prove that the Weaver was the better technique. However, by 1980 few were using the Weaver technique and Ross Seyfried was the last World Champion (1981) to use the Weaver style of shooting. There has not been a Weaver style shooter to finish in the top 18 positions of any IPSC match for many years.

It is ironic that many of those who promoted the Weaver based on its initial success within IPSC competition could not accept the Leatham-Enos technique when it clearly began to dominate the same sport a few years later. There are still many Cooper supporters (and some shooting academies) that insist on teaching the Weaver stance.

Notice arms are extended equally and head is tilted forward to look through the gun sights.

Presentation of handgun with sights under dominate eye.

So far we have talked mainly about the stance and have considered only two handed control of the handgun. At my school, we devote half of our instruction toward the use of one-hand control of the handgun. I tell my students that the handgun is way down the list of weapons I would choose to defend myself if I were pre-warned of an attack. The first several choices would be a selection of shoulder weapons.

However, there are several situations in real life that make the handgun superior to shoulder weapons. In most instances, if the shooter is involved in an activity that requires the use of one hand, the other hand can control a handgun better than a shoulder weapon. These situations include driving, climbing, repelling, crawling, close contact with the enemy, carrying something, or trying to hold a door or some other portal open while shooting. Of course there is also the case of a serious injury that may prevent the use of the support hand.

We find that when reviewing surveillance films that capture real gun battles as well as simulated battles, there are many times that people revert to one-handed shooting techniques even though they have not been trained to do so. The Leatham-Enos stance described before works well regardless of which single hand you choose to shoot with. Because both arms are extended equally, you can simply transfer the handgun from one hand to the other without changing your stance. Most of us choose to move our left foot back slightly farther than a two-hand hold when shooting with the right-hand and vice versa while shooting with the left-hand, but the position is a stable platform without moving anything.

Grip

How we grip the handgun is an important technique not only in allowing us to control the weapon better, but also to prevent malfunctions. Almost all modern handguns have a slide stop lever located on the frame of the pistol which is in close proximity of the shooters thumb. Most handguns have the slide stop located on the left side of the firearm but some have it located on both sides. In any case, the shooter must be careful not to place a thumb in such a way that it

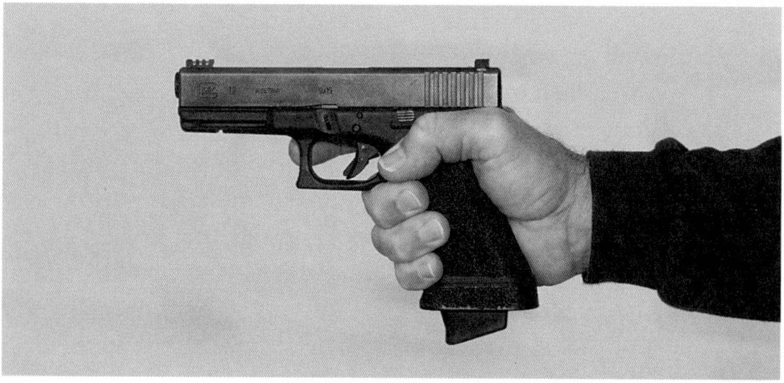

Strong hand grip avoiding slide stop.

Photo of two hand grip showing thumb crossing over of the support thumb and hand fitting like a puzzle.

touches the slide stop. The thumb does not have to hold the slide stop down; all it needs to do is to touch it while shooting, to prevent the slide from locking open on the last shot.

Over my 35 years of instructing I have seen hundreds of shooters complain about the pistol failing to lock open on the last shot, not understanding that it was their grip that was causing the problem. I teach that a right-handed shooter should have the thumb touch the middle finger when shooting one handed to prevent interference. When shooting with two hands, I insist on having the right thumb cross over the support thumb and place pressure on the support thumb's most rearward joint to prevent interference.

In two-handed shooting, the hands must fit together like a puzzle to insure the most contact with the surface of the grip. Placing the support thumb over the shooting thumb prevents necessary contact with the grip. The fingers of the support hand need to wrap around the grip of the shooting hand. Much of the strength of our grip is in the three fingers that oppose the thumb. The forefinger provides much of that strength and should be used to increase the clamp pressure on the handgun grip, and not out on the trigger guard. The support thumb should be aimed toward the target and it can rest on the frame of the weapon, but never allow it to rest against the slide. Review the picture of my grip on the previous page.

Spot Shooting

Now that we have an idea of the proper stance and grip of a modern firearm, we will proceed to learn how to train the subconscious to shoot and hit a small spot. Take an unloaded pistol into your dry fire safe area. Follow the rules as set forth in the dry fire chapter. Put a 2-inch diameter spot on the wall, about 5 feet from the floor and step back 15 to 20 feet

From this point on in the book, we will refer to the intended point of bullet impact as a "spot" and not a target. The term target is too general for reactive shooting. We must learn to direct our attention toward a finite spot on the target.

Before we go any further, we must determine which eye is our dominate eye. With both eyes open, focus on a small object or vertical element such as a post or pillar. Keep your face aimed squarely at the intended element and maintain focus on that element. Make a fist with your thumb extending upward. Quickly extend your hand out at arms length and cover up the post or the spot with your thumb. Without moving anything, close your left eye. If your thumb remains in line with the vertical element or the spot, then you are right eye dominate. If, when you close your left eye, you recognize that your thumb is instantly no longer in line with the element, then you are left eye dominate. If you have trouble doing this drill you are more than likely "cross-eye dominate." About 30 percent of the general population is cross-eye dominate, which is to say that they are right-handed but their left eye is dominate, or just the reverse.

If you turn out to be cross-eye dominate, place the firearm in the hand that is associated with your dominate eye. If you are left-eye dominate, you will grip the weapon and control the trigger with your left hand. I don't care how uncoordinated you think you are with your left hand, do not, I repeat, do not allow yourself to start training in a cross-eye dominate situation.

Now, extend the weapon out using a proper two-handed hold as I described in the section on grip and stance. Align the sights at a point where the wall meets the floor. Both eyes must be open and the pistol must be controlled by the correct hand aligned directly under the dominate eye. None of this will work if the firearm is not directly in line with the dominate eye. Align the pistol, using both front and rear sight, at the intersection of the wall and floor. That area of the floor will be a blur while the front sight will be crisp and clear.

Without moving the firearm, move your focus of both eyes to the spot on the wall. Now, the spot on the wall will be crisp and clear. Hold that position in anticipation of a start signal. With a single-action pistol such as a Colt 1911 or a Glock, place your trigger finger outside of the trigger guard and rest it on the frame or front of the guard. Upon a start signal, lift the pistol, engage the trigger, and complete the hammer or striker snap just as the sights align on the spot. Your focus will instantly transition from the spot to the front sight and the sight will become clear as the spot becomes a blur. This is all done simultaneously.

Just as the click occurs, freeze everything so that the pistol does not travel past the spot. Freeze every muscle including your trigger finger which has now forced the trigger against the trigger stop. All of the involved muscles must be tensioned just at the click. I call it "physical focus." Your body must be tensioned just as if you were striking a heavy punching bag or were blocking a punch when the hammer action clicks.

The good thing about the nature of the human system is that we can truly multitask. Gross motor skills (such as lifting the pistol to the spot) can take place at the same time as fine motor skills (such as pulling the trigger). At the same time we are lifting the pistol and pulling the trigger, we are also changing our focus from the spot to our front sight. To do this correctly, we must do everything simultaneously.

We need to complete the dry-fire just when our eyes identify that the sights will be accurately aligned on the spot. The dominate eye sees the front sight clearly while the non-dominant eye is aware of the spot. We must do all this in two response times, or half a second (0.5 seconds). If you put the shot timer on a par time of 0.5 seconds, you can barley distinguish a break between the start and stop signal. The hammer must fall before the stop signal chirps its final beep.

We start the firearm aimed well below the target for safety and tactical reasons. We quickly transfer our focus to the spot and upon the start signal drive the weapon to eye level while we transfer our focus to the front sight. We must learn this ability to acquire our sights so that we can later work from a holster or other starting positions.

Most people, with further directions given in a later chapter, can accomplish this task in less than 100 repetitions, provided they have the physical strength. If you are normally right-handed but are using your left hand to control the firearm because of a dominate left eye, it will probably take you more repetitions to get it correct.

A double-action pistol or revolver poses no additional challenge, although I teach starting with the finger in contact with the trigger but relaxed prior to the start. I teach this mainly because double-action pistols sometimes have safeties that disconnect the trigger and sometimes the pistol has transitioned to the single-action mode. By touching the trigger, the subconscious mind knows instantly of the condition of the trigger system of the pistol. This training could one day save your life.

Trigger Control, Flip and Press

If you lift the weapon to eye level, stabilize it, refine the sight picture, and then initiate the trigger press, much like a precision shot, your time will be around 1.25 seconds or longer. With our technique we must be able to fire an accurate shot in .5 seconds. However, to accomplish this we are not just lifting the weapon and pulling the trigger. If you did, the shot would probably occur before you were near the spot. I call it "working the trigger." You're loading up the trigger and it begins to move back as you lift the pistol, but you are timing the action without any pause so that the hammer falls at the very instant the sights align with the spot. This is why I don't recommend light triggers on weapons intended for reactive shooting. At the instant the weapon fires, the shooter should freeze the trigger against the trigger stop. Should a second shot be necessary, the finger instantly flips off of the trigger completely, almost rebounding off the inside surface of the front of the trigger guard, and an additional press of the trigger is initiated. We call this principal the "flip and press" at the Rogers Shooting School.

The process I have described above should not be confused with what we call "staging" the trigger. Staging a trigger is commonly used to make a precision shot. To stage a revolver in double action the skilled shooter quickly pulls the trigger to a point where the cylinder indexes with the cylinder stop and then the shooter pauses the action with the hammer at its fullest extension. The trained shooter knows exactly where this sweet spot is based on prior firing or dry firing. When the shooter's mind is satisfied with the stabilization of the target, weapon, and sights, the final action of firing the revolver is caused by a very small movement of the trigger and very light pressure by the shooter's trigger finger. The shooter has reduced an eight to 10 pound trigger pull with ¾" of travel to a final 3 pound or less trigger pull with less than 1/16" of travel. This same technique can also be used with double action and single action pistols. Instead of rotating the cylinder which does not exist with the pistol, the shooter learns to pre-load the trigger to a certain point and then pause the action. Depending on the actual firing mechanism, skilled shooters can control the trigger very reliably while staging the action. This process is used by most skilled shooters when making precision shots. However, it is not what I teach for making a reactive shot. The reason is that it takes too much time. The mind uses one response time to start the trigger pull while staging. It uses another response time to pause the action just prior to firing. It must now use another response time to reinitiate the final pulling of the trigger. What I teach only uses one response time and that is to start the trigger pull.

This is exactly the same technique that a baseball batter is using. He starts his swing upon the windup and delivery of the pitch. From that point on, he slows down, speeds up, or stops his swing based on what his eyes tell him. We are doing the same thing, except we are coordinating our arm and trigger finger movements with what our eyes are reading, so that the shot breaks at the instant of alignment and not a millisecond before or after. In the next chapter we will discuss the mechanics of how we learn a reactive skill.

Centering, Focal Attention, PIR and Follow-Through

Before we start, I must define some terms that I have used for over 30 years. Most of these definitions are of my own invention so you're not likely to find them in any dictionary or to have read them in a gun magazine.

"Centering" is the trained ability to coordinate some part, or parts, of your body with the use of your "Focal Attention." A baseball batter or a tennis player coordinates his swing by using his eyes so that the ball is accurately hit. "Focal Attention" is using the eyes in an intense manner to focus on a spot or a finite area of an intended target. It is the essence of the term "watch the ball" that is yelled out in so many sports by frustrated coaches.

"Positive Instant Recognition" (PIR) is the name I have given to the methodology necessary to learn any rapid eye-hand coordinated skill. You can swing at a thrown ball many times and if you miss the ball each time, you learn nothing. If, however, you hit the ball, you have a positive instant result. If you can hear, feel, and see that result within about 300 milliseconds of your successful action, the mind forms a "mental trace" or what would be medically called a "neural pathway."

This is somewhat like tracing a simple map on a piece of paper to get from one location to another, except it's the neural pathways along which your brain's signals pass that are learning to "read" the map. The subconscious mind must recognize a path from the inception of a stimulus to the successful solution to the stimulus— and capture that pattern in memory.

If your mind sees that same pattern again, it has a better chance of directing your arms, wrists, and hands in order to hit the ball. That path has been trod before and the nervous system "remembers" the way. As we repeat the process over and over again, we become more skilled, hence the phrase, "practice makes perfect." As they say in martial arts training, "Repetition is the mother of all skill."

In order to learn any eye-hand coordinated skill we must first have a positive event. You must eventually hit the ball in order to start the learning process of how to swing a bat. Next, we must recognize the positive event through our senses and, thirdly, the outcome needs to be recognized instantly.

Scientists have tested the learning ability of the subconscious mind and have concluded that the mind loses its ability to follow the "trace" back to the start of the action if it is not aware of the final result in less than 300 milliseconds. Swinging and hitting a "photon" ball, generated by a computer— but not knowing that you actually hit the ball until a second later— becomes a test of your present skill. You would not be able to improve your skill using this form of training. If you were to shoot at skeet targets that neither break nor change in any manner when hit, you would never learn how to improve your score. You would learn nothing from the exercise.

The most important part of the PIR learning equation is "follow-through." Follow-through is maintaining the physical action with our body and eyes well past the positive result so that our subconscious can form the mental trace, or neural pathway, of the entire event. If we were to try to teach a place kicker to kick a football through the uprights, but we put him in a helmet that automatically obstructs his vision just as he kicks the ball, it is obvious that he would never learn the skill. He may be following through with his body but without his eyes telling him where the ball is actually going, he could never form the necessary memory pattern to kick the ball through the goal

In the learning situation of shooting moving targets, the shooter typically comes from behind the moving target, establishes a lead and fires the shot. To learn the skill properly, the shooter should maintain the same lead, movement, and head contact with the shotgun while keeping both eyes fixated on the target well past the event of the target breaking. This insures that the mind can form the necessary picture, or the mental trace, of the event.

With the knowledge we now have, we can go back and describe the training of dry firing the spot on the wall in 0.5 seconds, as discussed in the previous chapter. The aligning of the weapon using the sights and aiming at the intersection of the floor and wall allows our mind to experience the feel of the weapon in our hands while it is aligned on something. We can look at a spot on the wall, close our eyes, and then accurately point our forefinger at that spot with our eyes closed. We can do this because through past experience our mind knows what that feels like.

A handgun is just an extension of our arm. In time we should be able to point the muzzle of our firearm as quickly and as accurately as we can our forefinger.

Why do I have you begin by pointing the firearm at the floor and not the spot? Would it not be better if we started the firearm aimed directly at the spot?

We have seen many times on TV when supposedly well trained police officers point a firearm directly at someone and command them not to move. Wouldn't this tactic insure our chances of a quick hit? The answer has several parts to it. The first reason is safety. In my instruction, I do not allow any movement of the muzzle toward an intended recipient of the bullet unless you have already committed yourself to that shot. Remember, in reactive shooting, you have already initiated the trigger pull well before the muzzle is aligned on the intended spot.

I ask every law enforcement group to which I have the opportunity to lecture, "What is the primary safety associated with every firearm?" Most will declare that the trigger finger removed from the trigger is that universal safety. The correct answer is muzzle direction. Never forget this simple rule. A muzzle pointed in a safe direction is, and always will be, your primary safety.

In order to disassemble a Glock pistol, we must first pull the trigger and release the striker. If we insist on aiming the weapon at our groin or foot each time we do that, we are taking a serious risk. Most states have laws that consider pointing a firearm directly at someone while threatening them as an "assault with a deadly weapon." Pointing the muzzle of a firearm at a police officer during a confrontation justifies the use of deadly force toward you by that officer.

So, why do many police officers aim their firearms directly at subjects when they challenge them? Because that is the way they have been trained. Their mind needs to see a stabilized target, a stabilized weapon, and a defined sight picture before they actually place their finger on the trigger, and all of this before they start the firing sequence. Remember, in our previous drill we learned to complete a firing solution in 0.5 seconds starting with the pistol aimed at the floor. Because of our ability to multitask, the response time to place our finger on the trigger and then pull that trigger, with the weapon eye level, is the same response time to lifting the pistol to eye level while pulling the trigger. In fact, one could learn to simultaneously side-step, lift the weapon to eye level to a designated spot while pulling the trigger, all in the same response time as just placing the finger on the trigger and then pulling it.

Another issue is more of a tactical concern. If you use a two-hand hold and bring the weapon to eye level aiming at someone, your view of the person's body below the weapon is obstructed. Their hand could be withdrawing a badge or a weapon from a pocket, but you would not likely see it. Aiming the weapon directly at someone ("locking out on the target") and issuing a stern command such as "Don't move or I will shoot" can create a very dangerous condition. The subconscious can be confused by such a subjective order.

In many cases during Simunition training, I have witnessed students under stress reacting to aggression from another subject involved in the scenario, and they often shoot the wrong subject. This "stress fire" situation is exacerbated if the weapon is already locked onto a non-hostile suspect or, in the case of Simunitions, a role player.

Finally, locking out on a target in a fixed and rigid manner usually prevents a hit on a target that suddenly moves. Years ago I designed a shooting drill that used a "falling man" cardboard target. When the target was tripped it would randomly fall right or left behind a steel guard. From the time the target was operated until it was behind cover, it was exposed about 0.75 seconds or enough time for two well-placed reactive shots.

During a match I ran about 40 IPSC competitors through the falling man drill. The start position was with the safety off, finger on the trigger, and weapon sighted at the target, which was about 7 yards away. A random time, very short, after the shooter stated "Don't move, or I will shoot," the target fell in a random direction. Hardly any shooter got a hit on the target. I cycled everyone back through a second time except I had them start their pistols aimed at a safe direction in front of the target with their finger off the trigger. After the same command and random operation of the target, most all of the shooters got at least one hit on the target.

You should be able to figure out why from what I have told you, but to be sure you understand, let me explain. We know from our test of tapping the shot timer after a signal that the fastest time for a simple response is 0.25 seconds. In the first scenario, the shooters were locked out and aimed at the target. Their mind knew exactly where the target was and they were ready to shoot at the instant the target moved. However, because of the response time, (the sum of reaction time plus movement time) they were not shooting at the target, but where the target had been 0.25 seconds earlier. In the second scenario, the shooters knew they were not prepared to shoot when the target moved. This required them to establish the direction and speed of the target before driving the pistol. The shooter's subconscious mind, through prior training, anticipated where the target was going and directed a timed shot to successfully intercept the target. For the reasons stated above, learn to keep the muzzle of your weapon pointed in a safe direction until you not only have decided to shoot something, but are actually in the process of shooting that something.

Now back to the training of our initial drill. I call this type of drill a "centering drill." You are teaching you subconscious so that you can coordinate the alignment and firing of the pistol by using your eyes. After you confirm the sight alignment of the pistol in a safe direction, well below the spot, you will direct your focal attention at the spot. You know that you could quickly point your forefinger at that spot so now you must learn to quickly point the pistol at the spot. Your mind can use a number of different references to align an instrument or tool. You normally start with the grip or feel of the item to align it. That is why we confirm the alignment of the front and back sight every time we extend the firearm so that in a short time our hands will know what the firearm feels like when it is aligned.

Next, we must learn how to develop our focal attention. Look at the spot intently. Close your eyes and try to visualize precisely where the spot is. Now look intently at the spot, close your eyes and quickly lift the firearm to where your mind thinks the spot is. Open your eyes immediately upon stopping the movement of the firearm but make your focus and focal attention rivet on the front sight. At this point, the sights should be in line with your dominate eye and close to alignment with the spot. Remember the PIR fundamentals. Your eyes need to recognize the results of your body's actions within 300 milliseconds of the completion of those actions. Do not be concerned that the spot is out of focus or even if you seem to see two spots when you focus on the front sight. Your mind knows exactly where the spot is because of the first focal attention. The firearm will be aligned toward the proper target even if a phantom target exists.

In less than 20 cycles, the sights should be aligned within about two-inches of the spot at 25 feet away. Now begin to do the drill without closing your eyes. You will learn that you start the centering drill just as before by placing your focal attention on the spot, but as you quickly lift the firearm you will transition your focal attention to the front sight as you look through the rear sight. I call it "looking through the gun."

You should be able to drive or steer the firearm at the last instant so that the sights align right on the spot. Remember, with the proper stance, torso and head arched slightly forward, you are extending the handgun under your dominate eye and bringing your head and eyes in a position to look through the sights. Your eyes transition at the last instant from the spot to the front sight. Your eyes need to be able to clearly define the front sight at the extended distance, which I will discuss later in a chapter on corrective lenses). Once you have accomplished this task, add the movement of the finger from the outside of the trigger guard to working the trigger, so that the hammer or striker falls at the instant the sights are on the spot. The PIR fundamentals are still necessary. We have a positive result when the sights are aligned and the hammer falls at the same instant. Now add the shot timer set to 0.5 seconds and practice until you are on the spot when the hammer falls and the time is within the 0.5 seconds.

Introduction to an OPE

We have just learned a crucial skill, how to dry fire an unloaded firearm and have the sights aligned on a two-inch spot at the instant the hammer falls, all in 0.5 seconds. Could we now load up with real ammo and reliably hit a two-inch spot at 25 feet away in 0.5 seconds? The short answer is no. Here's why.

I've taken numerous non-shooters through the two-inch dry fire drill until they were quick, smooth, and confident. I have then taken them to the range for their first live-fire session. After a dry fire warm up of the drill, I have cycled them through a magazine of dummy rounds with one live round somewhere near the bottom. What I have found is this: When the novice shooter finally fires the live shot and it is not anticipated, they almost always strike the two-inch spot. If I then load another live round in the pistol and have the novice shooter repeat the drill, they almost always miss the two-inch spot and usually the entire two-foot-by-two-foot cardboard that the spot was drawn on.

I make a point to ask each class why they think this phenomenon takes place. The answer usually is that the student is anticipating the recoil of the live-fire shot and pushes the gun down to counter the muzzle flip caused by the bullet exiting the barrel. Their timing is slightly off and they push before the bullet actually exits the barrel. This concept has been sold to millions of shooters and even has earned a name, "pre-ignition push." Unfortunately, it is nonsense.

What is really going on is more basic. I have named this phenomena an "over-pressure event" or OPE. I tell my students that teaching them to shoot is no more difficult than to teach them how to hit a ball with a golf club, baseball bat, or tennis racquet except when we hit a ball, it does not explode. We all are predisposed to flinch when an explosion occurs near to us. I believe it only takes one OPE in our life that is associated with pain or some type of injury to teach the subconscious that it wants no part of this loud, sudden, explosive noise ever again.

If you have gone for an eye exam in the last few years, you may be familiar with a machine that tests for glaucoma. You rest you chin on a ledge and an instrument is moved very close to one of your eyes. A small blast of air that you could barely feel on your finger is directed at your eye. If you have never had this done before, there is usually no anxiety involved with the test of the first eye. In every case, everyone blinks within one response time or 0.25 of a second from the small blast of air. There is usually a great deal of anxiety involved when you now have to place your other eye in line with the air blast. The doctor can assure you that your eye will not be hurt in any way and you can consciously order yourself not to flinch or to move your head or eye in any manner. But guess what? You will not only blink, you will jerk your chin away from the small blast of air every time it cycles. In fact, if you anticipate the doctor triggering the device, your head will be gone before the air blast.

Now imagine if you were pulling the trigger on the air blast machine. The subconscious mind that knows exactly when the air blast will trigger is the same subconscious that wants no part of the event. If you were holding the air blast machine in your hands, you would subconsciously push the device away from your face as you anticipated the blast. This is the same thing that happens with every shooter when they pull the trigger of a handgun that produces a concussion. It is the OPE that has confused shooting instructors for some 200 years and caused so much counterproductive training.

I'm sure that the first instructor who taught a student in the manner described above with dry fire was totally frustrated by the student's actions after the first live fire shot. At that point he probably ordered the student to stabilize the firearm, refine the sight picture, and slowly press-press-press the trigger for a surprise break. Sound familiar? It's the classic remedy for a flinch. But what is this type of instruction actually doing? By slowly pressing the trigger, we are trying to fool the subconscious mind in not knowing exactly when the firearm will fire. You will still flinch but the movement of the firearm is after the shot is fired.

You can further fool the mind by using very light triggers, but even with light triggers, the mind will finally have enough experience to know exactly when the weapon will fire. This entire phenomenon is a critical hindrance to learning any type of reactive shooting. Remember, in reactive shooting the mind is timing the shot and knows in a few milliseconds when the shot will fire. The subconscious mind that is timing the shot is the same subconscious mind that does not know how to deal with over-pressure. As a result of this neurological conflict, the shooter not only pushes the firearm away from his face when he knows the gun will fire, but also simultaneously blinks as part of the flinch reflex.

Many times the muscle memory of the shooter will return the firearm to the initial aiming point before the eyes are opened and re-focused. The improperly trained shooter is puzzled because he confirmed the sight picture before and after the shot, but the bullet impact is not on the target. Some have a very consistent flinch and can actually shoot a fair group on a target, although it is not on the spot.

Right-handed shooters most always push the handgun down and left while southpaws tend to push the handgun down and right. Because the firearm moves off the spot and the shooter simultaneously blinks, the subconscious mind can never have a proper follow-through to form a mental trace. Because most shooting instructors don't have a clue about what's really going on, they insist on talking the shooter through the time-tested course of stabilize, align sight, and press-press-press to get a surprise break. They end up spending weeks and thousands of rounds of ammo, and when their students finally finish the course, it takes them 1.25 seconds or more to hit somewhere on a humanoid size target at 10 yards. Welcome to the present state of standard firearms training academies.

How can we quickly fix this problem which is at its root caused by an over-pressure event? Easy! Just put a silencer on your handgun and in minutes you can have the novice shooter back to hitting the two-inch spot in 0.5 seconds. I have done this many times and it works great. There are just a few problems with that solution. Silencers are very expensive to legally own and are a serious crime if not legally papered and properly registered. Furthermore, they are a little difficult to conceal in your favorite inside-the-pants holster. 'What else can I do?" you ask. Well, I hope that's why you bought this book. Go to the next chapter.

Learning to Shoot a Reactive Shot

We now know a little about the ugly enemy, OPE. We need to learn more. Concussion, the force that disturbs us, is detected mainly through our eyes. The normal reaction to concussion before proper training is for the shooter to blink and push the explosion away from the face at the instant that the event is expected. The eyes are very sensitive to pressure. For years I have had people who would flinch during every reactive shot with a handgun. I could work with them dry firing and they could engage the moving targets in reaction time without flinching. I could work in a live round when they believed that it was a dummy and they would hit the spot in time. As soon as they went back to live fire, the flinch would reappear

In frustration, I would have them focus on a spot and then close their eyes before they raised the handgun and pulled the trigger. An amazing thing would happen. They did not flinch. Apparently when the mind believed that the eyes were protected by being closed, the subconscious was then not concerned about the concussion. I also discovered many years ago, totally by accident, that when we ran a drill wearing gas masks, the students shot better than without the mask.

Another thing to realize is that concussion dissipates in force by the cube. That is to say, the pressure wave is going out in every direction, not just down a focused linear path. The farther away our face is from the source of a concussion, the more comfortable we are. Even an inch makes a difference.

Rifles shooting a .44 Magnum cartridge are much less likely to cause a flinch than a short-barreled handgun shooting the same round. I have recently seen some very experienced shooters destroyed by shooting ARs and M16s with barrels shorter than an M-4 carbine. Without suppressors on these weapons, the shooters are in big trouble. I call the really short barreled 5.56 carbines Flinch-A-Matics.

Certain pistol cartridges are more difficult to shoot because of the intensity of the OPE. The .357 Magnum, .44 Magnum, and .40 S&W are three that instantly come to mind. Years ago, I taught my wife Christie to shoot handguns using reactive shooting drills that I had used to teach the Special Forces. She, like me, became an IPSC competitor and won a number of important matches. She was twice the women's champion of the Bianchi Cup. She was the U.S. Women's IPSC National Champion as well as the women's champion for several international competitions.

When she started competition, we both shot good old .45 ACPs. Later we all recognized the advantage of the .38 super, not just for extra round count, but also because the muzzle compensators worked so well. The .45 ACP was a relatively low pressure round. Venting the powder particles out in an upward direction did not really do much to compensate for the muzzle flip, but it helped. However, venting the high pressure of the .38 Super was a different matter altogether. To really make the "comps" work effectively and to also make major power factor, we eventually hot-loaded 130 grain bullets to maximum pressure. Christie shot the 160 grain .38 Super loads well but when we transitioned to the hotter loads and lighter bullets, she could not deal with the concussion and almost quit shooting.

Correct Repetition

Let's go over a few fundamentals of reactive shooting. The subconscious, based on prior repetitions of correct techniques, formulates a solution to a certain shooting problem and times the shot precisely as the necessary sight picture is acquired. That same subconscious, through prior experience, associates an over-pressure event with pain or injury. Since the subconscious mind knows exactly when the shot will fire, there is a great desire for the mind to cause the body to flinch just as the weapon fires. How do we teach the mind not to react to the OPE in a negative manner such as the flinch?

The answer is the same way we teach the subconscious to do anything. Correct repetition.

The following information is for a beginning shooter, but the same guidelines can be used for an experienced "precision" shooter to quickly learn the skills of reactive shooting. If you follow the guidelines, you can produce a skilled reactive shooter in a very short time and with little expense toward ammunition.

First, buy a good quality .22 revolver. I have had good results with Smith & Wesson. Some .22 firearms are damaged by dry firing so it would be wise to check your owner's manual before extended dry fire practice. All shooting and dry firing should be in double-action to learn how to control the action of smoothly rotating the cylinder.

The mind should learn that to control the trigger, it cannot just jerk away with the trigger finger. To pull the trigger on a revolver and rotate the cylinder in a rapid manner, without causing the muzzle to move, requires practice and should be done without ever firing a live round.

You can load the cylinder of your .22 with fired cases so that the firing pin will have something to impact against and not damage the firearm.

To begin with, some students will not even have the hand strength to operate a revolver smoothly in 0.5 seconds. You can start with the same spot drill that has been explained earlier in the book. The student needs to do the drill for a short period of time each day until hand strength and coordination have developed. On a start signal, the student must be able to lift the .22 revolver to eye level as the trigger is pulled and the hammer needs to strike instantly as the muzzle is on the spot. This entire action must happen within a 0.5 seconds time limit and the student needs to be able to do at least 12 times in quick succession.

All of this is done with the revolver being controlled by the hand that is associated with the dominate eye (as explained earlier) and with both eyes open. When this goal is met, it is time to go to a range. Remember, at the range all hits must be able to give the student instant feedback. You can shoot at Styrofoam dessert plates with a simple two-inch circle drawn in the middle or standard size copy paper with a spot drawn on it. You must not shoot more than about six shots per target so that your peripheral vision can instantly detect the hit. You must vary the height and distance of the targets so that you don't teach the subconscious bad habits.

If you were to learn how to shoot a sling shot or bow and arrow by placing a target at a certain distance and following the same type of training as described by this book, you would find that you could learn quickly how to follow through and hit the object. The learning process is much quicker than with a firearm because there is no concussion associated with the event and therefore follow-through is not interrupted. Your mind would quickly learn exactly what sight picture (or other necessary reference points) was required in order to hit the target.

If, however, after learning how to hit a target at a specified distance, you moved the target to a farther away position, you would not likely be able to hit that target the first few attempts. That is because the subconscious has learned only what sight picture was necessary for the close target. For this reason we must learn to shoot at objects that vary in distance, height, and size, and we must learn how to transition to these various challenges instantly. By placing targets at various distances and requiring yourself to engage these targets in random order, you can condition the mind to know precisely what is necessary to hit each target.

To begin with, keep the distance close but maintain the 0.5 second drill we've covered previously. Start with two targets at 10 and 15 feet and work out to 20 and 30 feet. Start first with .22 LR standard velocity or subsonic loads. Make sure to wear good eye and ear protection. Move up to .22 LR high velocity rounds as you become proficient. Use a shot timer like those made by Competition Electronics or PACT to keep the shot in the 0.5 second time frame.

Once you can consistently hit the two-inch spot in 0.5 seconds, advance to some of the higher velocity game loads that are available. At the same time you move up to high velocity .22 LR ammo that has a bit more pop and slightly more noticeable "explosion," add targets that react well when hit, such as potatoes, charcoal briquettes, balloons or clay targets. Seeing these targets dance or disintegrate is strong visual feedback and helps motivate you to follow-through. The pleasure of seeing something blow up is a natural way to entice you to follow-through and see the target explode, without flinching.

This is part of my whole program to train the subconscious not to react to an OPE caused by pulling the trigger of a weapon. As you become skilled with the .22 revolver you should move on to a center fire semi-auto pistol, preferably a 9mm. I highly recommend that you purchase a modern, reliable pistol that has the ability to change over the barrel and slide to a .22 Long Rifle cartridge. The Glock 17 has proven itself at our range as an excellent primary training weapon for this and other reasons. There are several companies that make .22 conversion units for the Glock 17.

Every drill that I talk about in this book should be accomplished first with a .22 conversion and then the center fire cartridge. By transitioning gradually to a cartridge that has greater concussion, you're conditioning your subconscious to deal with the over-pressure event. The final thing to remember about OPE is that it is a training problem. In a real-life situation when the adrenalin begins to pump through the body, we find that the subconscious deals with concussion by shutting down that part of the nervous system that is affected by an over-pressure event.

It is difficult for me to pattern a new 12 gauge shotgun. I put up a large paper target, step off the required distance and perform a precision-type shot. I may have to repeat this drill several times to insure that I have good data. By the third or fourth shot, I'm ready to stop. Under those conditions it becomes very difficult for me to fire a 12 gauge shotgun without a flinch. However, I've shot and hit 100 straight targets in a trap event and I've shot over 500 rounds in one day hunting dove in Mexico and never had a flinch. The point is that my mind only anticipates and shies away from the OPE in a training environment; out in the field with the birds flying, my subconscious is too enthralled with the excitement to be distracted with an OPE.

Most military and law enforcement agencies insist on training with the same high-pressure loads that they carry on duty. The thought is that the students need to be conditioned to the high-pressure round so that it will not adversely affect their performance in a real-life combat situation. A student must learn to control the recoil of his handgun with the round that he carries, but that can be accomplished near the end of a training program. The truth is that in a real-life combat situation, you could substitute a .357 Magnum for 9mm and the shooter would not likely know the difference.

Physical Focus

The position you have been working on is what I call the "extended ready, confirmed alignment" ready position. Its name describes the start position. We drive the weapon out equally with both arms. The support hand must fit the grip of the handgun much like a puzzle goes together, in order to get as much contact with the surface of the grip as possible. We are controlling the movement of the handgun in our hand, when it fires, by a frictional lock on the grip.

We must learn to lock up the muscles in our body so that the weapon has very little movement throughout the firing cycle. Almost every shooting discipline with the exception of IPSC, IDPA, or our type of reactive shooting is not concerned with the movement of the handgun after the shot is fired. In slow fire bull's eye, there's plenty of time to realign the handgun and take another slow shot. In our discipline of reactive shooting, we are concerned with the movement of the muzzle after firing. We must be able to follow shots or fire multiple shots with split times under 0.25 seconds and the bullets need to impact within a couple inches of the intended spot

I refer to this physical lock-up condition as "physical focus." You must learn how to instantly tension the muscles in your body just as the shot is fired so that the handgun does not appear to move. Whatever movement does occur needs to be consistent with each shot. The muzzle cannot move up and to the left one shot, and up and to the right the next shot. This is the advantage of using two hands. If you have applied equal force to the handgun with each hand and arm, the handgun will recoil in a uniform pattern. Once you learn physical focus, the handgun will move very little and that movement will be consistent between shots.

This skill cannot be learned by dry fire or any other means, other than shooting live ammo. It should be learned first with a .22 LR pistol and then a center fire cartridge such as a 9mm. As you learn how to control the 9mm, you can then move up to a .45 ACP and later the .40 S&W. By progressing in this manner, you're conditioning your physical strength at the same time you're conditioning your subconscious for the increased concussion associated with the higher pressure rounds.

Physical focus is best learned by shooting multiple shots with less than 0.25 of a second split times, while maintaining a three-inch group, at a distance of 10 yards from a target. First, learn to shoot doubles. Then shoot quads. When you can shoot four shots with split times less than 0.25 seconds, advance to six shots.

I developed a drill many years ago that tests the skill of physical focus. It is shot with a semi-auto pistol with at least seven rounds capacity. At 10 yards from a target that has a spot, chest high, and another spot at the head height, a shooter starts with the weapon at "extended ready." Upon the start signal, the shooter shoots six shots at the chest high spot and then one shot at the head-high spot. All hits must be inside an 8-inch diameter circle centered on the spots and the drill must be completed in less than 2.25 seconds.

This allows 0.5 seconds for the first shot, 0.25 second splits for five additional shots and 0.5 seconds to shoot the seventh shot on the spot at head height. It has been called the "Bill Drill" although the first "Bill Drill" was named after Bill Wilson and his drill of drawing and shooting six shots into a small circle as fast as possible. Again, as explained before, once you can accomplish this drill with a .22 semi-auto pistol, move on to a center fire semi-auto. Invest in some quality "dummy" or safety rounds for your center fire handgun. Every time you go out to practice, set up some drills that you can alternate a live fire shot followed by a dry fire or dummy shot. I find it works best when you have an alternating pattern and not a random situation. Set you timer to the half second limit and drill back and forth trying to improve your accuracy. Since your mind knows when a dummy round is coming it is more likely not to flinch. The more you do the drill without thinking about whether the gun will fire or not, the better your follow through will get. In time, with practice, your subconscious will finally not care if the gun fires or not, it simply wants to see the result of the shot.

The Transition Position

The "transition position" is a start position that I use primarily for training. Both hands are indexed properly on the grip with the trigger finger outside of the guard, just like the "extended ready position" for single-action pistols. The trigger finger must be outside the trigger guard regardless of the type of action.

Both forearms are parallel with the ground with the both elbows lightly touching your ribs. The slide and or barrel are also parallel with the ground and the muzzle is pointed in a safe direction down range. The handgun is aligned directly under the dominate eye with the controlling hand being on the same side as the dominate eye. I also call this a "rest" position because the shooter can stay in this position for a long time without tiring. I teach this position after the extended ready so that the shooter already has a subconscious alignment of handgun just by feel.

Upon a start signal, the shooter must simultaneously extend the handgun out toward the spot as the trigger finger moves into the trigger guard and begins to work the trigger. The shortest distance between two points is a straight line, so the muzzle of the handgun must travel in a straight line toward the spot without forming any arc. Just as the muzzle intercepts the spot, the dominate eye transitions from the spot to the front sight and the handgun fires.

There are actually two major actions going on at the same time. The mind has already given the order to pull the trigger at the same time it has given the order to extend the handgun, just like I described in the extended ready position. You cannot just pull the trigger instantly without totally missing the spot.

The controlling finger must start the action and work the trigger carefully while the arms and hands steer the muzzle to the spot. Even when the mind knows that the handgun is firing, the hands and arms are still steering the muzzle to the spot. It is like trying to drive a car at high speed through a narrow gate. You are still steering and controlling the car until you pass through the gate

This is also another way to explain the term follow-through. Remember you are steering or controlling the alignment of the handgun through the shot. The time I allow for a two-inch spot up to 30 feet away is 0.75 of a second. Over the years of testing the transition position, I have observed that an additional full response time (or 0.25 seconds) is required to deliver the same accuracy as the extended ready position.

Some instructors insist on teaching the transition, or a slightly modified, muzzle up position version, as a tactical position to use in certain situations. I do not agree with this instruction. In a number of tests over many years, this position has never been able to compete in speed or accuracy with the extended ready start position. The extended ready position with the muzzle directed toward the ground is also much safer than the transition position in case of an accidental firing of the handgun.

So why do I teach the transition position? Because it is a necessary skill to have in order to learn how to draw and shoot from a holster. You should only begin transition training after you have become skilled at the extended ready position. You must remember that after completing a shot or series of shots from the transition position, you should not quickly retract your arms and hands back to the transition position. This can become a serious bad habit.

At my range, each shooting cell has multiple targets that can randomly appear. I have witnessed many shooters who have been taught the transition position as a tactical starting point. They have not been taught follow-through and upon completing a shot, they quickly bring the handgun back into the transition position. In many cases they have not effectively stopped the attacking target, or there is another target that appears while they are retracting the handgun. They become totally ineffective at engaging the targets and their back and forth extending motion looks like they're sawing wood.

After any shooting event, which ends with the handgun extended, the shooter should continue to follow-through, looking through the handgun. The shooter should then slowly return to the extended ready position with the handgun pointed only as low as necessary to have a clear view of the battlefield. Practice these principals as you continue to shoot your .22 revolver at the two-inch spot and transition to a semi-auto .22 pistol. Change the height and distance of the spot and include reactive targets like potatoes, and clay targets. Then transition to a center fire pistol. At this point, I must caution you not to begin to "point shoot" at the spot.

Point Shooting

Point shooting is a term I mentioned earlier in the book, something I was taught in the FBI. The skill and methods of teaching point shooting have been around for over a 100 years. Two British Army officers, William Fairbairn and Eric Sykes wrote a training manual during World War II to teach British commandos the skill of point shooting. Many books and articles have been written since and a large number of institutions teach point shooting as the primary skill for CQB, or close quarters battle.

With point shooting (or a related form of unaimed fire known as hip shooting), the shot is fired without reference to the sights. The most popular technique of point shooting is for the shooter to extend the handgun out with the slide or barrel aligned under the shooter's nose. The shooter looks over the handgun and his focal attention never leaves the target. This type of training uses the same methods as I discussed earlier in the book. The shooter can quickly learn how to align the muzzle by feel. The shooter's peripheral vision can accurately align the handgun horizontally, especially if the slide or barrel is several inches long, but the vertical alignment is controlled strictly by the feel of the grip.

In a short time, novice shooters can learn to hit a six-inch spot up to 20 feet away. If your instruction has followed my guidelines, you will have trained yourself to steer the handgun at the last instant by looking through the sights. If you begin to practice point shooting, you will begin to look over the handgun and focus only on the target. With some success, you will begin to retrain the subconscious.

The mind quickly loses the trained skill of looking through the sights as the shot breaks and in a short time it becomes totally dependant upon the feedback caused by the bullet striking the target. Point shooting has a limit when it comes to accuracy. Without the steering feedback information provided by visual reference points of the handgun, including the sights, the human body can only rely on how the handgun feels when the shot is fired. Even the most skilled point shooters fail when it comes to hitting small partial targets at distances greater than 30 feet.

What I'm teaching is totally different. My students are looking through the handgun. Their subconscious minds learn precisely what references they must have in order to hit a specific spot. At close distances, the mind will accept alignment of the handgun based on a fuzzy view of the slide superimposed on the target while at farther distances, it will require a more refined sight picture of the rear and front sights.

Your peripheral vision confirms a hit to begin with, but in short order the mind knows precisely where the bullet should impact by reading the flash sight picture just as the weapon fires. Studies have proved that the mind captures and sees a picture up to 200 milliseconds after the picture is gone. With this type of training, the mind relies on the feedback of the flash sight picture not on the bullet impact. In a real-life gun battle, the bullet impact is seldom witnessed, even though the shooter's eyes may be focused on the intended enemy.

Even with thousands of rounds of training, point shooting skills fail as the target gets smaller or the distance gets farther away. Police officers trained in this manner can usually hit a man-sized target at distances up to 10 yards away but fail miserably to hit the subject in the right eye as he returns fire over the hood of a car.

Some proponents of point shooting insist that the human eye cannot transition its focus from the subject to references on the handgun under the stress induced by combat. There has been no evidence of this in any study and the concept counters what is seen in competitive sports including IPSC and IDPA shooting events, as well as real-life gun battles.

Some believe that as the body transitions to the full-blown transformation of Condition Red, advanced heart beat, elevated blood pressure and the effects of adrenalin compromises the ability of the eyes to change focus. The truth of the matter is that a majority of handgun battles start and are over before the body has a chance to undergo the 7 to 10 seconds necessary to be affected by the physiological changes that take place under stress.

Over the years we have had a number of skilled point shooters attend my shooting school to try and prove that their technique is equal to or greater than reactive, sighted shooting in CQB scenarios. To date we have never had one of these shooters pass our basic score. Ed McGivern, one of the greatest exhibition shooters to ever live, was skilled at point shooting and reactive sight shooting. He, however, relied on reactive sight shooting when doing all of his aerial demonstrations. He was capable of shooting six one-inch glass balls, thrown in the air simultaneously, with solid .38 Special bullets fired from an S&W revolver. He relied on a flash sight picture for each shot to accomplish this feat.

As was proven to me by Ken Hackathorn and I in turn proved to the FBI, point shooting is no faster than reactive sight shooting. We can only move our arms and hands in human response time. The eyes, on the other hand, can gather steering information much faster than the body can react to that information. The eyes can watch a movie with frame speeds of 24 frames per second. The mind records and interprets these images clearly at that speed. Therefore, the eyes could see six separate sight pictures during the fastest time that the finger could pull the trigger. The eyes, however, must be able to "look through the weapon" and not over it in order to receive the necessary steering information.

Point shooters insist that their method is quicker than sighted shooting. This is because they are comparing point shooting to the skills of someone taught incorrectly to begin with. To the average academy student who has been taught to shoot their fastest shot in 1.5 seconds, due to thousands of rounds of "precision" shooting, point shooting is definitely faster. But in test after test, point shooting cannot compete in speed or accuracy with what I am teaching.

Those taught the system of point shooting have trained the subconscious to look over the handgun intently at the target in order to receive the necessary feedback. Once they train the mind to this type of visual reference, this method is a very difficult habit to break. We can point to the failure of point shooting in numerous gun battles at close distances, where subjects were using cover or had hostages, and were only offering partial exposure. In real life it is difficult or impossible to see the hits on an adversary during the combat situation.

Students who arrive at my shooting school with point shooting skills have a very difficult time making the transition. They can usually improve their point shooting skills to hit the head target at 25 feet in 0.5 seconds but they cannot take that skill to the next level and hit the head of the hostage situation at 30 feet in 0.5 seconds. When their system fails, they begin to rationalize their failure by stating that in real gun battles, a human's eyes cannot use steering references associated with the handgun. However, evidence does not support their case.

Drawing from a Holster

We have taken you step by step from the extended ready through the transition position with your trusty .22 revolver, then your .22 semi-auto conversion pistol, and then with center fire cartridges. You have probably shot 1,000 rounds or more and dry fired three times that amount, always using your shot timer to keep you on pace with reaction speed. You have learned how to "work the trigger" quickly but smoothly so that the muzzle does not wobble as you complete the action. You have learned to look "through the handgun" and read what ever flash sight picture is necessary to hit a two-inch spot from distances of 5 to 30 feet. You can hit the spot in 0.5 seconds starting from the "extended ready, sights confirmed" and in 0.75 seconds starting from the "transition position". It is now time to learn how to draw.

Some instructors teach the draw as a series of numbered steps. That is counterproductive and a waste of time. With complex holsters, we sometime break down the release of securing devices in steps, but the actual skill of drawing is a smooth, continuous operation and it should be learned just that way. There should only be a slight pause in the whole sequence and that is when the shooter reaches the initial index point. The initial index point is where the shooting hand makes first contact with the handgun, holster, or both and recognizes this point as the beginning of the draw.

The first action of the draw is for the controlling hand to move toward the index point as the support hand simultaneously moves to a position slightly above the waist and close to the body, directly under the dominate eye. The support hand should be slightly cupped with the fingers toward the body. If the holster you're using doesn't have any securing straps or other retention devices, such as an open-top holster, the index point should be the actual shooting grip that you have been perfecting.

There should be a momentary pause to insure that this starting point is as near to perfect as possible. If your holster has a securing or retention device that prevents movement of the handgun, it is necessary to index the hand to the position that is most efficient to start the unlocking procedure. Every different holster design has its own index point and it is necessary for the shooter's hand to identify this position before continuing the draw.

Without a slight pause to insure this proper index point, the entire drawing sequence can be destroyed, ending up in a totally botched draw and sometimes even a dropped handgun. From the index position, the fingers of the controlling hand unlock any mechanism that secures the handgun in the holster. A well-designed holster should, as part of the design, allow the hand to travel continuously from the unlocking position to the final shooting grip of the handgun.

Once the shooting grip has been established, the handgun must be moved in a manner to draw it from the holster. Some of my older holster designs required that the handgun be rocked forward or, in later designs, rocked backward before the handgun could be lifted from the holster. In any case, the design must allow the shooting grip to remain constant during the draw.

The shooter should practice lifting the handgun while maintaining "almost-contact" between the side of the pistol with the shooter's torso until the muzzle has cleared the top of the holster. The elbow should be directed straight back and not allowed to drift outwards. Continue to lift the handgun straight up until the lowest part of your hand is a couple inches higher than the latitude of your naval. Without allowing the muzzle any downward motion, the handgun is rotated as if pivoted at the grip so that the muzzle is pointed downrange, or in the direction of a threat.

The finger is still out of the trigger guard at this point. Now the handgun and controlling hand moves slightly diagonal, almost maintaining contact with the body until it is directly aligned with the dominate eye. At this point, the support hand completes the two hand hold and you are now in the transition start position.

You must not pause at this position! If you are drawing with the intention of making an immediate shot, you will continue through the transition position. Your trigger finger will transfer to the trigger and you will begin to work the trigger as you drive the handgun out under the dominate eye.

The proper transition position, with the slide or barrel parallel to the ground, should allow the shooter to fire at any phase of the extension and hit an adversary that has closed the distance with the shooter. If the adversary has maintained enough distance to allow full extension of the handgun, then the handgun should be brought to eye level as the shot is completed.

Follow-through and additional shots (as necessary until the threat is neutralized) should be completed before slowly bringing the handgun muzzle down to the extended ready position. If the threat is not imminent when the shooter decides to draw, the shooter should proceed through the transition position to the extended ready position with his sights confirmed before searching for the threat.

If the threat is dissipated or nullified, the shooter should check the condition of his handgun to insure that it is fully loaded and all safety conditions are met before returning the handgun to the holster. While training on the range, do not leave your position with a partially loaded weapon with the intention of placing a loaded magazine into the holstered weapon at a later time. Remember the subconscious does not understand logic or strategy. It only knows what it knows through constant and consistent repetition. Leaving a secure position with your firearm only partially loaded is a bad habit to get into.

The same spot drills that you have used for the extended ready and transition positions can be done from the draw, with a goal of 1.25 to 1.50 seconds time limit, depending on the security devices that are necessary to release before drawing. If you are training to prepare yourself for a concealed carry license, you should practice with the firearm, holster, and clothing that you intend to wear when you are carrying on the street. You should always learn the draw by working with your holster and an unloaded firearm. Be sure to follow the dry fire safety rules as recommended earlier in the book.

Corrective Lenses for Shooting

I was able to shoot consistently high scores on the standard test at my school for many years until I turned 55. During the season that I turned 55, my scores became inconsistent and on average went down around 10 percent. I suspected that the problem was with my eyes since I had to really force my dominate eye to see the front sight clearly.

I had talked to other shooters who had experimented with a technique called mono-vision. Essentially, you have one eye corrected so that in a relaxed condition it can see close-up clearly while the other eye is set to see at distance. The mind sorts things out in such a short period of time that you can see clearly at both distances with both eyes open.

The problem is that most eye doctors insist on correcting the dominate eye to see clearly at distance. This is just the opposite of what a shooter needs. I asked my wife Christie to accurately measure the distance from my dominate eye to the front sight of one of my pistols with my arms fully extended. With this measurement in hand, I went to my optometrist and requested him to correct my dominate eye so that in a relaxed state, that eye could see clearly at the measured distance. At first my optometrist wanted me to reconsider and correct the non-dominate eye. I explained my situation and he agreed to make the correction.

With a new pair of light weight polycarbonate shooting glasses corrected so that my dominate eye could see the front sight clearly, my scores immediately improved and at age 59 I actually shot the first, and at the time, the only perfect score at my range. My recommendation is that if you cannot see the front sight clearly without squinting, it is time to correct the problem. The same thing can be done, I'm told, with Lasik surgery.

Shooting On Steel Targets

Shooting on steel targets is the most efficient way to learn reactive shooting skills, but there is always the inherent risk of being injured by bullet fragments. To reduce the chance of injury shooters should always wear good protective eye wear. There are also a number of common sense rules to follow to minimize your chances of injury.

If you can, use fragmentation rounds. If you do not have access to fragmentation rounds, try to use solid bullets that have a plated copper covering instead of a true copper jacket. Do not shoot jacketed hollow point bullets on steel. The jacket separates in an unpredictable manner and can return toward the shooter. Do not shoot hollow base bullets like shotgun slugs or .38 wad cutters used in PPC matches. The bullets collapse much like a well designed race car and the entire bullet can bounce back toward the shooter.

Always shoot perpendicular to the surface of the steel targets. Shooting at an oblique angle toward the surface of a steel target can cause a ricochet. The bullet does not fragment but acts much like a billiard ball and is only deflected in another direction. It still maintains its mass and much of its energy. For this same reason, never shoot at a steel target that has craters or dimples. If you hit the edge of a dimple it is like shooting the steel at an angle. The bullet does not fragment but remains intact and can return toward the shooter.

Steel targets should be constructed so that bullet fragments formed at the face of the target are not redirected toward the shooter. A lip, edge, or foot which is perpendicular to the face of a target can redirect the splatter toward the shooter. When a solid bullet impacts a smooth hard steel surface at a true right angle, it will disintegrate into small particles. The particles are traveling at high speeds but they do not have much mass. They lose energy quickly and are not dangerous past about 25 feet.

Most of those particles exit parallel to the surface of the face of the target. However some particles can come back up to a 45 degree angle. The returning splatter forms an ever increasing cone so that the shooter is normally safe, but someone standing on the same shooting line near the shooter can be hit with the high speed particles. For this reason the targets should be baffled so that only the shooter can see and shoot at the face of the target. The rule of thumb for an observer is that if they can see the face of a steel target that is not perpendicular to their viewpoint, they can be hit with fragments.

The Second Amendment

It is my belief that all law-abiding and mentally sound citizens of the United States should be taught responsibility and basic familiarization with firearms. It should be part of our public education system. Even to this day, all able-bodied men of Switzerland are trained and considered part of the country's "armed militia" with their military-issue weapons stored at their homes. This mindset has kept the Swiss free from enemy occupation for centuries. We as American citizens are ultimately responsible for the security of our homes, neighborhoods, towns and cities. We are endowed with the responsibility of keeping our country a free nation as set forth by the United States Constitution.

Our founding fathers fought King George for our independence, but they realized that freedom is not free and it is a very perishable commodity. The Second Amendment was placed in our constitution so that citizens could remain armed in order to defend themselves against any tyrannical government.

Today we live in a very liberal society. Many in our government talk of world unity and peace through negotiation. They have a socialistic agenda which will necessarily limit individual freedoms while it empowers the government. Socialism must rely on taking by force the wealth of high achievers and re-distributing it to the masses who in turn keep the government in power. As the system begins to fail, it is necessary to take more wealth away from the middle-class since the upper-class has already been destroyed.

At this point, the government must be concerned about a rebellion. They cannot afford to allow the citizens to be armed in a manner that they could pose an effective resistance to the government. Historically, every nation that has proceeded down this course has been disarmed. We have seen most of Europe, Australia, and our neighbor to the north, Canada, confiscate their citizen's firearms in the name of safety and controlling "violence." Disarming honest citizens has never decreased crime and has always required more government security forces to intervene which is the intended purpose to begin with.

Many of our present government officials want to ban anything that looks like a military or assault weapon on the grounds that these weapons are not used for sport or hunting. The Second Amendment was not written to protect hunter's rights or any type of shooting sport. It was specifically written to protect the ownership of "assault weapons." Richard Henry Lee, the man who drafted the Bill of Rights, put it thus: "A militia, when properly formed, are in fact the people themselves. ... The Constitution ought to secure a genuine [militia] and guard against a select militia, by providing that the militias shall always be kept well organized, armed, and disciplined, and include ... all men capable of bearing arms, and that all regulations tending to render this militia useless and defenseless, by establishing select corps of militia, or distinct bodies of military men not having permanent interests and attachments in the community [are] to be avoided. ... To preserve liberty, it is essential that the whole body of the people always possess arms, and be taught alike, especially when young, how to use them."

These aphorisms, found on the Internet, echo the same theme in more modern language:

I don't carry a gun to kill people.

I carry a gun to keep from being killed.

I don't carry a gun to scare people.

I carry a gun because sometimes this world can be a scary place.

I don't carry a gun because I'm paranoid.

I carry a gun because there are real threats in the world.

I don't carry a gun because I'm evil.

I carry a gun because I have lived long enough to see the evil in the world.

continued

I don't carry a gun because I hate the government.

I carry a gun because I understand the limitations of government.

I don't carry a gun because I'm angry.

I carry a gun so that I don't have to spend the rest of my life hating myself for failing to be prepared.

I don't carry a gun because I want to shoot someone.

I carry a gun because I want to die at a ripe old age in my bed, and not on a sidewalk somewhere tomorrow afternoon.

I don't carry a gun because I'm a cowboy.

I carry a gun because, when I die and go to heaven,
I want to be a cowboy.

I don't carry a gun to make me feel like a man.

I carry a gun because men know how to take care of themselves and the ones they love.

I don't carry a gun because I feel inadequate.

I carry a gun because unarmed and facing three armed thugs,
I am inadequate.

I don't carry a gun because I love it.

I carry a gun because I love life and the people who make it meaningful to me.

I hope this book has given you some training concepts that will allow you to teach yourself or someone else how to effectively engage a relatively small target in less than a second with a handgun at distances less than 60 feet from the target. I can only hope that the administrators responsible for police and military training will read this book and change the way they teach basic firearms training. The past and present basic instruction of "point shooting" or "precision shooting" has cost our service personnel many lives in real combat.

Reactive shooting should be taught first and the student will naturally transition to precision skills as greater accuracy is required by moving the target farther away.